SAVING SOULS

SAVING SOULS:
THE STRUGGLE TO END THE
TRANSATLANTIC TRADE IN AFRICANS

A BICENTENNIAL CARIBBEAN REFLECTION

HILARY McD. BECKLES
VERENE A. SHEPHERD

With a Foreword by the Most Honourable P.J. Patterson

Ian Randle Publishers
Kingston ● Miami

First published in Jamaica, 2007 by
Ian Randle Publishers
11 Cunningham Avenue
Box 686
Kingston 6
www.ianrandlepublishers.com

© 2007 Hilary McD. Beckles and Verene A. Shepherd

National Library of Jamaica Cataloguing in Publication Data

Beckles, Hilary McD.
    Saving Souls: the struggle to end the transatlantic trade in Africans : a
bicentennial Caribbean reflection / Hilary McD. Beckles, Verene A.
Shepherd; with a foreword by the Most Honourable P.J. Patterson

    p. :   ill. ;   cm

    Bibliography : p.

    ISBN 978-976-637-307-8 (pbk)

    1. Antislavery movements – Great Britain   2. Antislavery movements –
Africa, West 3. Slavery – West Indies   4. Slaves – Emancipation
5. Slave trade – West Indies
    I. Shepherd, Verene A.   II. Title

    326.8   dc 22

Cover and book design by Ian Randle Publishers
Printed in the United States of America

CONTENTS

List of Illustrations

List of Figures

List of Tables

The commemoration of significant moments in Caribbean history is a long-standing practice in the region. Each CARICOM country celebrates Emancipation Day and Independence Day. Others mark Indian Arrival Day, the 'Encounter' and the birthdays of national heroes and heroines. While some of these historical moments are national events, marked in individual states, others, like Emancipation Day, provide the region with an opportunity to exercise its collective memory and unite around a celebratory moment in regional history.

Regional solidarity was also expressed in 2004 when we celebrated the Haitian bicentennial and recalled the regional emancipatory logic of Haitian leaders expressed through their offer of safe harbour for fleeing enslaved people from existing slave regimes and anti-slave trade activism long after they had cemented their own freedom and independence through revolution and the defeat of the French and allied forces.

While external action in 2004 threatened to destabilize the celebration, regional support for deposed President Jean Bertrand Aristide and to resolving the political problems in our sister CARICOM nation testified to our commitment to Haiti's continued freedom and keeping alive the memory of the slavery experience in the shaping of our modern nations.

As I stressed then, as Chairman of CARICOM, Haiti has passed through decades of political turbulence and we have a responsibility to end its isolation.

As we did in 2004, so we do now in 2007: rally around a significant historical moment in Caribbean history. The year 2007, the bicentennial of the legislative abolition of the Transatlantic Trade in Africans (TTA) by Britain, will provide the Commonwealth Caribbean with an opportunity to reflect on and explore openly its historical relationship to the TTA, slavery and its legacies. Above all, it will create a space within which the Caribbean public can be introduced to the story of abolitionism from the perspective of the descendants of those who endured the Middle Passage.

An important aspect of that discourse on abolition which must be disseminated, especially to our youth, is that the first efforts to end the transatlantic trade in Africans and, indeed, slavery, were made by the victims of the trade themselves and not by British humanitarians, missionaries and political activists.

Within recent years, as Clare Midgely has observed, scholars have started to acknowledge that the origins of British anti-slavery resided in black resistance within Britain; that it was resistance

> which sparked the first white action in the form of a series of attempts by Granville Sharpe in the 1760s and 1770s to make slavery illegal within Britain and to use *habeas corpus* to secure freedom of individual enslaved persons.[1]

Despite this recognition, the accounts of the anti-TTA movement produced for Caribbean consumption have tended to accord primacy to the work of white, male abolitionists (despite the presence of many women in the struggle) and not acknowledge what is emerging now as an interaction between black self-emancipation and the humanitarian, legal and political struggles of whites.[2]

Of course, the black anti-slavery activists, especially those in Africa and the Caribbean, made no clear distinction between the abolition of the trade and the abolition of the slave system; and this indistinct line between what some see as two distinct movements may be responsible for the inability of some to name black anti-TTA heroes/heroines other than Olaudah Equiano,

Ignatius Sancho and Ottabah Coguano. But the activism
and the resilience of leaders of anti-slavery wars, for
example Tackey and Tomboy of Antigua; Pompey of
Exuma Island, The Bahamas; Ben and Cuffee of
Barbados; Black Tom, Sarah Bassett and Cabilecto of
Bermuda; Cuffee of Guyana; Boukman and Toussaint
L'Overture of Haiti; Nanny, Takyi and Blackwall of
Jamaica; Chatoyer of St. Vincent and Sandy of Tobago,[3]
need to be acknowledged as we embark on
commemorative activities.

Resistance to what was essentially a crime against
humanity was carried out by black people everywhere:
in Africa, on the Middle Passage, at the ports of arrival
in the Americas, on the plantations, in the Plantation
Houses and in England, where many were taken as
personal servants by their owners who were rich enough
to shun precarious tropical life for a more luxurious
existence in the metropole. Of course, such luxurious
life was made possible by the sweat and tears of enslaved
African men and women, two to four million of whom
were captured and forcefully relocated in the British-
colonized Caribbean. Colonial plantations, industrial
enterprises and mercantile enterprises based on the trade
in Africans, as many scholars have indicated, were major
sources of aristocratic wealth.[4] The rich West India
Interest was predictably resistant to the idea of abolition.
That is why Africans had to pioneer the anti-TTA
struggle.

The forms that resistance took varied and ranged
from marronage, manumission, and malingering to
destruction of property, strikes, labour bargaining and
outright war. Whether the plot was a minor or a major
one, no Caribbean territory was immune from the anti-
slavery struggle of enslaved Africans. This is indicated
by Michael Craton's research: two in The Bahamas in
1734 and 1787; eight in Barbados between 1649 and 1701;
nine in Jamaica between 1760 and 1806; and five in

Tobago from 1770 to 1807.[5] The Haitian revolution and Haiti's commitment to regional emancipation also created political instability in the region. By 1806 it was obvious to the British that the TTA had to be phased out, leading to the first step, the Order-in-Council legislating the step-by-step abolition of the TTA to the 'ceded territories'.

The Caribbean needs to find appropriate ways to honour those anti-slavery heroes/heroines who gave their lives to support an ideal and who paid the ultimate price so that life could be better for their descendants, so as to complete the project of iconic decolonization. As Professor David Trotman has observed, iconic and iconographic decolonization require 'political willingness, cultural awareness and financial resources'.[6]

Despite the challenges, the authors and supporters of this publication as well as the leaders of the bicentennial commemorative planning committees across the Caribbean must press on with their efforts to educate Caribbean people about a past which, while painful, provided important lessons about how our ancestors overcame adversity and left us a cultural legacy that has sustained us through trying times. After all, as Elsa Goveia observed insightfully as far back as 1959, 'knowledge of the past must play its part in our liberation from the bonds of the past'.[7] I urge civil society, CARICOM governments, the private sector and cultural agencies to join hands in marking a momentous event in the history of the African Diaspora and renew regional efforts to insist that those who committed this crime against humanity should make amends to the descendants of its victims as an act of final reconciliation.

Above all, let us endorse the sentiments expressed by the people of Ghana and enshrined in a plaque on the wall of the entrance to the male dungeon at Cape Coast Castle in Ghana:

May those who died rest in peace; may those who return find their roots; may humanity never again perpetrate such injustice against humanity. We the living vow to uphold this.

Percival J. Patterson
Former Chairman of CARICOM
Former Prime Minister of Jamaica

August 2006

Notes

1. Clare Midgely, *Women Against Slavery: The British Campaign, 1780–1870* (London and New York: Routledge, 1992), 10.
2. Ibid., 11.
3. Michael Craton, *Testing the Chains: Resistance to Slavery in the British West Indies* (Ithaca: Cornell University Press, 1982), 335–39.
4. Clare Midgely, *Women Against Slavery*, 10. See also Eric Williams, *Capitalism and Slavery* (Kingston: Ian Randle Publishers, 2004).
5. Craton, *Testing the Chains*, 335–39.
6. David Trotman, 'Symbolic Decolonization' (Text and Testimony Collective Keynote Lecture, Barbados, December 2004).
7. Quoted in Woodville Marshall's 'Foreword', in *Inside Slavery: Process and Legacy in the Caribbean Experience*, ed. Hilary Beckles (Kingston: Canoe Press, University of the West Indies, 1996), vii.

Preface

The Transatlantic Trade in Africans (TTA) has no equal in the annals of modern history in terms of the scope and depth of suffering experienced by its victims, mostly at the hands of European traders and enslavers. Yet, denial and silence continue to surround this human tragedy. Despite the silence, and because of the denial, its impact continues to be felt today in all corners of the world. The ideologies of race and colour that the slave system spawned in the sixteenth century that featured colonial societies built around notions of white supremacy and black inferiority continue to haunt human relations more than a century after abolition and emancipation. Denial and silence, furthermore, has meant that the true nature of this human tragedy has not been scientifically evaluated and assessed.

The bicentennial of the legislative abolition of the trade is now upon us; and in the Caribbean — a modern civilization, crafted and sustained by the horrors of the experience — civil society is preparing to mark this anniversary. The region will probably find itself doing so from a perspective that speaks to resistance, survival, and the triumph of human decency over destruction and despair. Respect for the social worth of free souls, and the celebration of the dignity of citizens, have replaced the selling of souls and the degradation of labour. Citizenship and nationhood have emerged from the ashes of chattel enslavement, and the right to life is embedded in laws that once served only the white and wealthy. Nevertheless, the bicentennial will also provide the Commonwealth Caribbean nations with an opportunity to revisit this tragedy and address the silence, even at the risk of opening painful wounds.

This text, like its companion, *Trading Souls*, is a reflection upon a history that was terrible and turbulent. It tries to make sense of the silence and denial even as it seeks to break it. Several developments inspired its emergence, although two were paramount: the establishment of National Bicentennial Commemorative Committees across the former (or still) British-colonized Caribbean (the first one established in Jamaica in December 2005 by the government of Jamaica and chaired by Verene) and those Committees' commitment to public education through the generation of educational material; and the initial mandate given to us by the University of the West Indies' Strategy Committee to lead the institution as it sought to find appropriate and meaningful ways to mark a moment in world history. Despite hiccups along the way, as two Caribbean historians conscious of the knowledge that inadequate attention is given to the project of reviving the life journeys of victims whose memory have either been erased or marginalized within manuscripts, we embraced the task of ensuring that hiccups would not destabilize an important mission.

The fact that we both journeyed from the bowels of the rural peasantry to the University of the West Indies (UWI) added a special dimension to the deliberation. We have no choice but to sing our peoples' song; their songs of pain but also of freedom. The words set forth are now free to chart their own passage. We celebrate the stance of our academy, governments and all cultural workers that know and promote the lessons of this history. It is not simply an academic, empirical, bicentennial polemic; neither is it a fresh marking in the mud that hides the heavy feet of men, women, and children, who were dragged across the Atlantic Ocean having exited through the door of no return. Is is an essay on the bicentennial of the 1806 Order-in-Council and 1807 Abolition Act. To facilitate easy reading, especially among students, we have tried to make it is less structured and more fluid in its texture. While we have benefited enormously from the pioneering work of colleagues like Robin Blackburn, Michael Craton, Philip Curtin, David Brion Davis, David Eltis, Elsa Goveia,

Barry Higman, Joseph Inikori, Paul Lovejoy, Hugh Thomas, and Alvin Thompson, and cite them extensively, we have dispensed with end/footnotes and opted instead for a selected bibliography. The function of this book is to speak, simply and clearly, about the fragments we have found upon the sands of a vast ocean that reveals details of the deaths it has known in small, unshapely portions. The trade in Africans across the Middle Passage will continue to haunt and to tell. As historians our objective is to find and show.

This reflection, then, offered as an exhibit in a discourse now 200 years old, may disturb feathers rather than settle dust. We offer it hopefully as a small truth against the mighty lies of time. If it urges further thought upon a past that will make for a better future, then we will be satisfied with the worth of our effort. Either way, it is presented by two descendants of survivors, and offered for all those who, despite the burden of this past, are still keeping the faith.

We thank Grace Jutan for help with typing and offer our sincere thanks to our student research assistants on this project: Dalea Bean (UWI), Nadine Hunt (York, Canada) and Tracy-Ann Johnson (UWI). We thank Daive Dunkley (University of Warwick) and the High Commissioner for Britain in Jamaica, His Excellency Jeremy Cresswell, for accessing copies of the Order-in-Council and the Abolition Act from the British House of Lords; the CHASE Fund (Jamaica) and UNESCO (Caribbean) for assisting with publication costs; Kay-Dean Lazarus (UWI), and the Jamaica National Bicentenary Committee's education sub-committee for editorial assistance; and the staff of Ian Randle Publishers for working with an impossible deadline in order to get the text ready for the bicentennial.

Hilary McD. Beckles
Verene A. Shepherd
August 2006

Introduction

*Knowledge of the past must play its part in our liberation
from the bonds of the past.*
                                    – Elsa Goveia, 1959

It is now generally accepted that the forced transportation of over 15 million enslaved Africans to the Caribbean and the wider Americas, the permanent dislocation of over 30 million in communities across the continent, and the mutilation and murder of millions unknown, constitute modernity's greatest crime against humanity. It remains puzzling, however, that Western European culture, while aggressively championing the cause of human liberty, political freedom, and the public accountability of government, should have promoted and globalized for near 400 years racialized black chattel slavery. Societies everywhere have known a variety of insidious crimes, but none has been as corrosive of the concept of humanity, as the evil represented by the centuries of chattel enslavement of Africans by Europeans in the Atlantic world.

One third of the African souls sold into slavery did not survive the Middle Passage but met watery graves or were fed live to fish. Others who tilled the fields and softened the soils with their blood now lie beneath the rubble of decayed and abandoned sugar estates, the cold hills of coffee estates, the pollution of cattle pens, and unknown cemeteries of old, unyielding cities. Their spirits, however, have remained as restless as the ocean that brought them hither. Day by day, fragments of memory are washed up upon our shores, like songs in search of willing lips.

It was materialist greed that motivated this crime against humanity. From the end of the fifteenth century to the end of the nineteenth century, the labour of enslaved victims, in addition to that of their progeny, contributed significantly to the economic modernization and cultural transformation of the Atlantic world that became home to the first transnational industrial complex. The enormous contribution made by the slave trading system to the development of Britain and other European countries has been more fully presented for critical assessment. Few scholars, in contrast, have followed where Walter Rodney led, illustrating the devastating impact of the transatlantic trade upon the development path of the West African economy and society. More energy has been directed at studying the slave system on the American side of the Atlantic and the process of abolition. This latter theme will be explored as both the former colonizer and the formerly colonized prepare to mark the bicentennial of the passage of the British Slave Trade Abolition Act of March 1807, in 2007. Caribbean historians have a responsibility to tell the story of abolition so that it reflects the contributions of the victims of the trade, even while acknowledging the critical role of British abolitionists in the abolition movement.

The process of terminating the highly profitable European transatlantic trade in African peoples was long, and drawn-out. Although Africans, including the enslaved, had long resisted its operation, abolition has traditionally been presented as a benevolent act by the British state that acquiesced under the mounting pressure of the intellectual classes and the political advocacy of religious and humanitarian activists. For this reason, elements in the UK will no doubt honour the humanitarian and political heroes of the Transatlantic Trade in Africans (TTA) abolition movement in 2007. Admittedly, there is substantial literature that details this rich history of British humanitarian and political opposition.

The British started in 1783 with the House of Commons debating an Abolition Bill. Those in favour of the Bill used predominately moral, religious, and philosophical arguments. They spoke of man's inhumanity to man, God's creation of all creatures, black and white, and the responsibility of the white race to uplift other races by moral example and ethical leadership. The majority in parliament, however, did not feel the weight of such propositions, and opposed the Bill on grounds that the trade and the colonial economy it supported were vital to the well-being of the white race and its nations.

Five years later, in 1788, the 'Committee for Effecting the Abolition of Slave Trade', was founded and led by Thomas Clarkson. The society agreed on a two-phased approach to achieving the abolition of the trade. First, it would seek to end the English trade in Africans by means of legislation; and second, it would move to gradually abolish slavery itself. In 1804, the year that Haitians declared independence from France, the House of Commons passed the Slave Trade Abolition Bill, but it was thrown out by the House of Lords. The following year, when the new Haitian Constitution provided that slave trading and slavery were crimes, the British Prime Minister, William Pitt, secured an Order-in-Council for the abolition of the trade. It provided that as of 1806, the new Caribbean Crown Colonies — Berbice, Demerara, Essequibo (modern day Guyana) and Trinidad — would not be allowed to import enslaved Africans (especially to start new plantations).

In January 1806, Charles Fox, Pitt's successor, moved a resolution for the immediate and total abolition of the transatlantic trade in Africans but no Bill was passed in that year. The Slave Trade Abolition Bill was eventually passed in the British House of Lords by 41 votes to 20 on March 25, 1807. In the House of Commons it had been carried by 114 to 15. The Bill became law in May 1807 to be effected by January 1, 1808 except where ships had already been cleared to trade in Africans. Such ships would be allowed to operate until March 1808.

So, the British led the parliamentary campaign. But no other European nation made as much profit from the trade. The Portuguese may have shipped more Africans but the British extracted the greatest per capita profits from the trade. This economic circumstance also determined the intensity of the British campaign.

Pride of place in the global abolition campaign has traditionally gone to the ideological and political strategies of British and European leadership while the organizational and political role played by black communities in Africa and in the Caribbean who were strongly committed to abolition has been marginalized. The campaign to end the transatlantic trade in Africans to the region cannot be separated from the resistance struggle of the Africans themselves. Blacks everywhere focused their politics upon both aspects of the crime against humanity — the trade and slavery itself. Their opposition to the trade was widespread in Africa, during the Middle Passage, and in the colonies. On winning their freedom in 1793, and assuming political power over the colony of St. Domingue (modern day Haiti), self-liberated blacks immediately abolished slave trading and slavery. In addition, they made it a criminal offence and refused to acknowledge the slave trading rights of European nations.

The 1805 Constitution of Haiti, for example, reflected the thinking of an entire nation. It provided automatic freedom and citizenship to any enslaved black person who arrived in Haiti. This legal facility effectively abolished slave trading and slavery for the first time in the Caribbean, replacing them with liberty, citizenship, and nationhood for all blacks. This was the most significant development for enslaved people in the wider Atlantic world. Enslaved people from all societies in the Caribbean and wider Americas fled to Haiti in search of freedom. During the early nineteenth century, the boat people across the Caribbean were in search of haven in Haiti. For this reason, Haiti became the Atlantic and global symbol of black freedom and liberation.

Overview of the Trade

Trading Souls shows in greater detail, that the Transatlantic trade in Africans (TTA) — the largest involuntary human migration in recorded history — was lucrative, maybe the largest commercial enterprise of its time. European nations went to war against each other in order to dominate the market. Recent research has suggested that over 15 million enslaved Africans were captured and shipped against their will across the Atlantic Ocean to the Americas between 1492 and 1870. As profits soared, and atrocities multiplied, no individual, government or group of people anywhere was able to stop its expansion. It engulfed everything and everyone within the Atlantic trading system.

Chattel enslavement, one of the most extreme forms of human bondage, had long been removed from Western Europe when the TTA emerged in the aftermath of Columbus's 1492 invasion of the Caribbean. The east Atlantic islands of Madeira, Azores, and Canaries, were colonized by the Portuguese and Spanish 40 years earlier, and enslaved West Africans were used in the colonial encounter. At this time, slave markets in Islamic North Africa and the Mediterranean were disposing of enslaved people drawn from many races and ethnicities. Spanish and Portuguese colonizers, then, were already accustomed to using the labour of enslaved Africans.

The Caribbean experience, however, was different to the Mediterranean and the East Atlantic islands. It witnessed the removal of other ethnicities from chattel enslavement and confined the relationship entirely to Africans. The 'Africanization' of the trade in enslaved people was something altogether new. As such it was a radical change from traditions of slave trading in the sense that it became associated almost exclusively with African peoples.

Only African people were denied indefinitely the right to life or social identity, and classified legally as property, chattel, and real estate. The TTA formed the backbone of British industry and commerce for the better part of the eighteenth century. It was the lifeline of the colonial economy in which British entrepreneurs grew to maturity as international financiers, bankers, insurance providers and brokerage agents. The TTA and the slave system supplied the financial energy and sustenance for major ports, enabling the mercantile elite to transition to the aristocracy.

The Caribbean was the principal market for the British TTA. The debate over the numbers of Africans shipped to the Caribbean still rages, but recent quantitative data indicate that the region accounted for 42 per cent of the estimated 15 million. Of the British colonies in the region, Jamaica, followed by Barbados, accounted for the majority of the total. For the period 1655–1857, Jamaica and Barbados received 11.2 per cent and 5.1 per cent respectively of the total trade, compared to 4.2 per cent for the Guianas and 3.2 per cent for the British Windward Islands and Trinidad combined.

Over two million Africans lost their lives in the capture, storage and shipment across the Atlantic — maybe another three million died within five years of arrival in the Americas. The brutality combined with other factors led to a demographic disaster. Millions of those who survived the Middle Passage died young. The magnitude of the tragedy can be effectively comprehended by adding the 15 million people exported to the Americas to the 30 million who were dislocated, dispersed and destroyed within the continent.

The TTA exported from Africa, not just an enormous pool of involuntary, victimized labour, but a wide range of intellectual, technical, scientific, and cultural resources. Africans took with them to the colonies an array of agricultural and manufacturing capabilities, as well as artistic and social ideas that gave the Caribbean much of its present identity. In fact, these cultural 'imports' informed and shaped significantly what later became known as 'New World Civilization'.

Meanwhile, Africa suffered the effects of the brain drain and militarization associated with the 'guns for slaves' exchange arrangement. In addition to consumer goods, most Africans were exchanged or sold for horses, textile, spirits, and firearms, a process that increased the military capabilities of indigenous elite clients. Many African societies were transformed as a result. Old states were subverted and destroyed, and new ones formed as elites vied to become clients of European slave traders. The changed political landscape of West Africa, from the mid-sixteenth century to the mid-nineteenth century, had more to do with this development than any other single factor.

The TTA stimulated African domestic political conflict. Increased levels of warfare weakened the potential for economic development. The political survival of states, and the ability of the elite to maintain their authority, soon depended on engagement with the trade. This process in turn created specific conditions for their own subversion, decline, and destruction. In effect, the masses of people were victims in the client relationships kings and nobles established with the heavily armed European slavers.

When communities recognized the extent to which their leaders were compromised and corrupted by the trade, they developed independent, mass-based resistance strategies against them and their European business partners. The TTA, then, created a long-term political circumstance in which the military superiority of European slavers and their African clients criminally victimized millions of people.

But captured Africans and many African communities did not collaborate with the project of selling black souls.

Indeed, Africans did not wish to be sold into slavery across the Atlantic and protested whenever they could.

Resistance in Africa and on the Middle Passage

Resistance effectively indicates how Africans as individuals and communities fundamentally rejected their entrapment and sale. The evidence of resistance in Africa and during the Middle Passage — from individual actions to collective armed revolt — has been under-researched despite the adequacy of enabling records.

According to David Eltis, popular opposition took several forms and was shaped by complex forces in different places over time. His analysis also points to a determined effort by some elite Africans to contain geographical encroachment and settlement by Europeans, in order to determine and limit the scope of their control over slave trading. In some instances such political action is posited as part of the resistance culture endemic to West Africa. More importantly, however, from the perspective of the enslaved, was their individual and community resistance to both African and European participants. The TTA — despite the recruitment and supply role played by elite Africans — was imposed upon African village communities by means of violent terror. The existence of many forts and castles, initially European monuments to trade and self-defence, evolved as symbols of terror forming a chain link along the West African Coast.

Resistance to enslavement within the TTA took different dimensions from traditional forms of social protest in West Africa. Chattel enslavement was an unfamiliar system of social oppression. Racist European notions of black cultural inferiority, and the implications of their enslavements laws, were not accepted by African communities which were resistant during capture and sale, on ships, and on arrival in the Caribbean.

Despite this oppostion, Europeans were able to establish trading arrangements with many West African kings and nobles. Philip Curtin's research has shown that some elite Africans restructured their systems of governance because of their new interest in the TTA. He has shown also, that the development of a client relationship with European traders became the economic foundation of some new states. Client governments raided neighbouring societies for the procurement of people to enslave. Such states, described by Curtin as predatory, increased their business efficiency over time. Adaptation to economic dependence on slaving almost always involved the creation of large armies that unleashed violence on neighbouring communities and beyond.

European slavers sometimes found it necessary to sponsor directly and indirectly organized violence against communities in order to secure persons for purchase. Client states sprung up within the vicinity of forts, and also in the interior. The Bambara state of Segu, formed about 1712, has been described as 'an enormous machine to produce slaves'. Raiding for captives and trading were crucial to its structure and behaviour. The Europeans provided guns to its leaders who supplied enslaved people.

Robin Law has shown, for example, that for about 20 years after the Dahomey conquest of Ouidah in 1727, the king sold large numbers of military captives to the Europeans as they were all considered his personal property. Soldiers surrendered all captives to the king after a military campaign, and received monetary payment. The royal monopoly of trading in Africans with Europeans could not generate enough captives to meet the demand. This forced the king to resort to purchasing people from independent raiding agents for resale to Europeans. African subjects, whether they lived within or beyond such client states, were exposed to the raiding forces of professional warriors. From Sénégal to Angola, these new states sprung up or were recreated from old states. One of their primary functions was to subvert and displace states and their leaders that were opposed to the TTA. Communities however, learnt how to defend themselves within this new context, and developed a culture of resistance against both the European and African collaborators.

In 1730, for example, Captain Adrien Vanvoorn, Dutch slaver and owner of the *Phoenix* from Nantes in France, and Laville Pichard, its captain, considered themselves and their crew quite safe at the mouth of the River Volta. Pichard was in the process of negotiating the purchase of people from a client king of a river community. Without warning, a group from the community appeared, burnt the ship as it was docked at Keta, and killed dozens of the crew.

Captain William Potter of the ship, *Perfect*, a Liverpool slaver, had a similar experience in 1758 on the River Gambia. His crew and ship were attacked by the community who witnessed the sale of some of its members. He had almost completed the purchase of over 300 people and was preparing for sail. The entire crew was killed in the assault. Ten years later, Hugh Thomas noted that the ship, *Côte d'or*, a 200-ton vessel belonging to Rafael Mendez of Bordeaux, in France, was assaulted on the River Bonny by warriors in rafts. Heavily armed with guns and knives, they boarded the ship, and freed the captives; the crew escaped when the Africans fled on seeing the approach of an English vessel.

The records of the English Royal African Company are replete with incidents of resistance on rivers and the coast. In 1703, for example, there is an account of Africans overpowering the guards in its fort at Sekondi, the Gold Coast, and beheading its supervisor. Also that year, a reference was made to the capture of a European agent in Anamabo who was forced to buy his life for all the money he had available to purchase Africans. In 1752 the *Marlborough*, a Bristol Ship carried 400 Africans from the Gold Coast. After a few days, 28 of the enslaved men found themselves on deck and seized muskets and killed all but eight of the crew, which numbered 35. This was but one incident among many. According to S.I. Martin, many protests took place. These happened mainly while ships were off the African coast or preparing to disembark. Shipboard protests were usually harshly suppressed by whippings, mutilation and even forced cannibalism of co-conspirators.

The 1999 database compiled on the TTA by Eltis and David Richardson et al. contain references to 382 shipboard revolts, two-thirds of which took place at the port of lading or within a week of setting sail. It is possible to identify the African region of departure for 342 of these revolts. When revolts were put down, the result was oftentimes reflected in high fatalities. According to Eltis, an average of 57 Africans per incident died in 18 revolts on ships in the Senegambia region compared to 24 per incident in 49 revolts elsewhere on the coast.

There are many detailed descriptions of revolts that took place during the early stages of the Middle Passage. In 1776 for example, an English Captain, Peleg Clarke, described how Africans aboard his vessel which had just lifted anchor at Accra rose up, struggled with the crew, and jumped overboard. Twenty-eight men and two women drowned, but six survived and were recaptured.

In 1765, Captain Hopkins of the *Sally* arrived in Antigua and told the story of an insurrection aboard his vessel four hours after leaving Calabar in the Bight of Biafra. The chained men were vomiting from seasickness, he reported, and were allowed on deck. A few healthy ones were allowed to cater to them, but conspired to secure the freedom of the entire group. The struggle to take the vessel took several hours. Captain Hopkins reported winning and forcing 80 Africans overboard to their deaths.

The Middle Passage was as violent and bloody a place as the plantations. According to Eltis:

The vast majority of rebellions resulted in inordinate bloodletting, whatever the outcome. If the slaves got the upper hand, even temporarily, most of the crew could expect to be killed. If the crew retained control, the death of the rebel leaders was almost inevitable, and the actual numbers of slaves put to death would be limited only by the need to get enough slaves to the Americas to ensure a profit in what was a highly competitive business.

Physical force determined who would control the ship; any relaxation of vigilance or reduction in the amount of force available to the crew could mean rebellion. It was a life and death struggle on both sides.

The captain of a Danish vessel, *Fredericius Ovartus*, suppressed an African insurrection on board. He dismembered the captives' arms, then legs, over a period of three days in full view of the rest of the captives. On the fourth day, their heads were cut off. A French captain who successfully quelled a rebellion on board his ship, hanged the rebel leaders by their feet and whipped them to death. A Dutch captain who survived a revolt hanged an Ashanti rebel leader by his arms after cutting off his hands; he was allowed to bleed to death in the sight of other captives.

While hundreds of similar occurrences were reported, some events had greater impact on the conduct of the trade than others. One well-documented event took place at Calabar in 1767. Seven English ships, five from Liverpool, one from Bristol, and one from London, were awaiting captives on the Old Calabar River where captains and agents had established trading relations with nobles in New Calabar. An armed contingent of over 30 Africans from Old Calabar attacked the English but were

unsuccessful because the king's soldiers assisted the
English. The leader of the Old Calabar warriors was
beheaded and survivors sold into slavery in the
Caribbean.

Descriptions of resistance to slaving on the West
African coast particularly in the forts are also quite vivid.
They depict circumstances in which Africans sought every
opportunity to free themselves. In 1727, for example,
enslaved Africans succeeded in organizing a rebellion in
the Dutch fort, Christiansborg, on the Gold Coast. They
fought Dutch soldiers, and killed the manager of the
fort. Many were able to secure their freedom, but those
who were injured in battle, and seized while the Dutch
regained control of the fort, were put to death by being
broken on the wheel. Their bodies were beheaded and
thrown into the sea, as was the customary punishment
for rebellious captives in the barracoons.

Europeans in Africa, like their counterparts in the
Americas, believed that beheading the bodies of Africans
before throwing them into the sea was the most effective
way to stamp out the practice of suicide. Europeans
thought that some Africans believed that at death the
soul returned to the ancestors for rebirth. By beheading
the African, Europeans sought to impress upon Africans
that there would be no journey to the ancestors since the
head was separated from the body and was disposed of
separately.

But suicide as an act of resistance was commonplace.
In this way, Africans sent a message to slavers that left
no doubt about the depth of their anti-slavery sentiments.
Hugh Thomas cites evidence pertaining to a case
experienced by slavers of the Dutch West India Company
in 1767:

A harsh response followed a sale of Ashanti slaves in
Elmina.

Six captives had been personal servants of a recently dead director-general of the . . . company, and they would have been freed if the Asantehene had paid some debts which he owed the company. But he did not, and the Dutch decided to sell the men concerned to traders. "We put their feet in shackles", . . . on the day that they were to be sold; the slave dungeons were thoroughly searched for knives and weapons, but apparently not enough.

What transpired at this stage horrified the Dutch, but was consistent with the defiant conduct of Africans in captivity. The narrative of this event continues:

The result . . . was that when the company slaves were ordered into yards to hold each other, they (the personal slaves) . . . cut their own throats; one negro even cut the throat of his wife and then his own; the yard of the noble company's chief castle was thus turned into a bloodbath.

The Atlantic voyage continued the violent warfare between captives and their captors. Furthermore, Michael Gomez finds that enslaved Igbos resisted enslavement and their new life in the United States south by committing suicide, and were commonly referred to as 'flying Africans'. Igbo people scattered throughout the Caribbean — especially in Jamaica — possibly demonstrated similar behaviour. Gomez argues that enslaved Africans saw 'flying suicide' as a means to return to Africa, their homeland. Maximum security was therefore the order of the journey. Slavers used the terror of guns and cannons mounted on deck pointing at the holds where captives were stored to secure order. Africans were always vigilant and expectant. The records of the Dutch West India Company list 15 major revolts aboard ships in the years 1751–75, most of them occurring, says Robin Blackburn, while the vessel was still close to the

African Coast. Thomas tells us that at least one insurrection per eight to ten voyages occurred on Dutch vessels, and one for every 25 voyages with the French slavers.

In 1751, Africans aboard the *Middelburgs Welvaren*, escaped the enchainment and engaged the crew in a battle. There were 260 on board. The captain, recognizing that the Africans had the advantage, ordered the cannon on board to be used against them. When the battle was over 230 Africans had been killed. On another occasion, captives aboard the ship *Vigilantie* in 1780 overpowered the crew and took control of the ship; the crew fled in lifeboats leaving the ship which was eventually captured by an English warship.

In 1770, the Africans aboard the Dutch slaver, *Guinniese Vriendschap*, led by one Essjerrie Ettin, seized control of the vessel but were soon overpowered by the Dutch warship *Castor*. In 1795, captives seized control of the *Neptunius*, and were seeking to return to Africa. An English warship alerted to the situation, and noting that it was not an English vessel, opened fire and blew the ship and the rebellious Africans out of the water.

Slavers were not keen to report accounts of successful African rebellions. But a few such cases exist. One of the earliest incidents was reported in 1532. It concerned the Portuguese captain, Estevão Carreira, of the vessel *Misericordia*. Carreira was transporting 109 Africans from Saõ Tomé to Elmina. Somehow, the Africans freed themselves, killed all the crew except the navigators aboard, and vanished. The navigators were freed, and reached Elmina in a lifeboat. The Portuguese heard no more of the ship, or its cargo.

The 1752 story of the *Marlborough* of Bristol had a similar ending. The 400 captives on board, from Elmina on the Gold Coast and Bonny on the Niger Delta, rose up and killed 33 of the 35-member crew; two were kept to assist with navigation, and were ordered to return the ship to Bonny. On the way to Bonny, the Gold Coast Africans objected to the destination, and a clash between the two groups ensued in which 98 persons were killed. At the end of the conflict, the Gold Coast group took control of the vessel, and headed for Elmina with one of the white navigators. They too vanished from written history.

Figure 1.1
Revolt on Board a Slaver, 1787

Source: http://oregonstate.edu/instruct/phl302/distance_arc/locke/locke-slavery-lec.html

Africans, then, did not wish to be captured, enslaved, and sold as a commodity. Despite the extensive record that speaks to the client relationship which elite Africans entered into with European traders, there is considerable evidence that details the nature of widespread community resistance. In the end, all Africans, whether in their roles as suppliers, client traders, ruling class collaborators, or captives, were adversely affected by the TTA.

African and Caribbean
Abolitionists in Action

Blacks on all sides of the Atlantic were the first to launch attacks on the trade in African peoples. African advocates in England were involved in the abolition movement and worked alongside white abolitionists. Ignatius Sancho for example, went to England in 1731, at the age of two. Believed to be the first African to vote in Britain, he was a free man and made a living as a shopkeeper. But it was his writings that established his reputation as a public figure. Sancho became the first African prose writer to have his work published in England. He also composed music and entertained famous characters of literary and artistic London. Sancho campaigned against the transatlantic trade in Africans and was known as an influential speaker. Sancho died in London on December 14, 1780. Many of his letters, for example, *Letters of the Late Ignatius Sancho: An African, to which are Prefixed, Memoirs of his Life* (1st ed., 2 vols. London: John Nichols, 1782) revealed his anti-TTA stance.

Figure 2.1
Ignatius Sancho

Source: http://www.aaregistry.com/african_american_history/2485
Ignatius_Sancho_an_early_Black_ American_writer___

Above all other African advocates Olaudah Equiano, or Gustavus Vassa (c.1745–1797), emerged as the quintessential African abolitionist. He was allegedly kidnapped in what is now Nigeria at the age of 11 and sold into slavery in Barbados and then to a Virginia planter. He later described how he was bought by a British naval officer, Captain Pascal, and later sold to a Quaker merchant.

Figure 2.2
Olaudah Equiano (Gustavus Vassa)

Source: http://www.brycchancarey.com/equiano/index.htm

After buying his freedom, and settling in England, he wrote and published his autobiography, *The Interesting Narrative of the Life of Olaudah Equiano, or Gustavus Vassa the African* (1789). It became an immediate bestseller and is today a classic in radical literature. Equiano travelled extensively around Britain giving talks about the evils of the transatlantic trade in Africans (TTA), and collaborated with Granville Sharp on a number of issues.

Ottabah Cugoano also publicly lobbied for the TTA's abolition and for emancipation. He was the first published African critic of the trade. Born in what is now Ghana, he was kidnapped and enslaved in the Caribbean. Cugoano migrated to England from Grenada around 1752 and was given his freedom. In his book, *Thoughts and Sentiments on the Evil and Wicked Traffic of the Slavery and Commerce of the Human Species*, published in 1787, he argued that enslaved people had both the moral right and the moral duty to resist and strike for freedom. He said:

> If any man should buy another man and compel him to his service and slavery without any agreement of that man to serve him, the enslaver is a robber and a defrauder of that man every day. Wherefore it is as much the duty of a man who is robbed in that manner to get out of the hands of his enslaver as it is for any honest community of men to get out of the hands of rogues and villains.

Even more than the literary works of these men, however, a growing number of blacks (upward of 15,000) were present in London and gave their support to the abolition movement.

Letters to newspapers entitled 'Sons of Africa' signalled that the black community was literate and politically active during the late eighteenth century. The testimonies of some of those enslaved were exposed by abolitionists to whip up public support for abolition. Other black abolitionist activists including Robert Mandeville, Thomas Cooper, Jasper Goree and William Greene also made their mark on London.·

The decision to abolish the trade in Africans was also influenced by the stirrings of blacks in the Caribbean. The emergence of Maroon communities, the successful Haitian Revolution, and other resistance movements prior to 1807 led parliamentarians such as Henry Brougham to argue that continuing the TTA would lead to more unwanted rebellious activity. As Brougham said:

When a fire is raging windward, is it the proper time for stirring up everything that is combustible in your warehouse and throwing into them new loads of material still more prone to explosion? Surely, surely, these most obvious considerations only have to be hinted at to demonstrate that independent of any other considerations against the Negro traffic, the present state of the French West Indies rendered the idea of continuing its existence for another hour worse than infamy.

Resistance in the Caribbean: The African Diaspora Continuum

From the outset the masses of African people turned their minds and faces against the trade in Africans. The anti-slavery movement of the Americas continued the struggles that took place in Africa and on the Atlantic Ocean. Throughout the slavery world, the radical tradition, with respect to justice and liberty, was inspired and informed by black resistance. As a result, for 400 years the dominant political features of all colonial societies were fear of African resistance the development of multi-faceted systems of defence against resistance, and the creation of socio-cultural institutions to exclude blacks from civil society. Keeping blacks in slavery, against the background of mass protest, became the priority objective of all colonial administrations. But the Pan-African movement that secured the decolonization of Africa in the mid-twentieth century was an embrace and validation of this deeper, wider history.

No colonial slave society was politically stable. Africans resisted wherever they were enslaved, and anti-slavery conflict was the order of the day. The record of anti-slavery actions in the colonies, from Canada in the north to Argentina in the south, is an impressive narrative of popular, democratic demand for civil rights and freedom. The Africans knew, of course, that the TTA would not end until slavery itself was abolished; they drew no conceptual or political line between the two. The TTA was the lifeline of slavery for most of the period. Resistance to both unjust systems was therefore endemic. Africans gave to the Americas this unrelenting impulse to struggle for human rights and democratic freedom. By promoting freedom as the principal political ideal in all colonies, blacks rooted within colonial societies the historic mandate demanded by Enlightenment thinkers in Europe. Everywhere, the words 'freedom' and 'liberty' were associated with the anti-slavery politics of blacks. They were the ones who gave these political concepts, real, popular, social meaning for working people.

The history of African anti-slavery politics in the Americas has received considerable attention in recent years. Hundreds of rebellions and wars have been studied as individual events, and within comparative contexts. Scientific attention has been paid to the following:

- African and Creole origins of leaders and their ideas
- the social and political ideologies that informed resistance
- the organization and planning of resistance activites
- successes and failures of rebellions and wars
- impact of protests upon civil rights reforms
- the rise of Haiti and Maroon communities as societies that represented black autonomy and self determination.

The literature demonstrates that the commitments of blacks to anti-slaving was irreversible despite heavy losses in terms of human life and immeasurable suffering. It also shows that the struggle for freedom and justice continued long after the Europeans took measures to constitutionally remove the institution of slavery from their colonies.

The enslaved Africans of St. Domingue defeated slaveholders on the battlefield during the 1790s, losing some 50,000 lives in the process. They declared national independence in 1804, renamed their country Hay ti / Ay ti, the indigenous name for the island they partly occupied, and abolished both the TTA and slavery. This was a unique and visionary development which set globally the nature of black expectations.

Haiti was the first country where enslaved Africans were able to hold and exercise formal political power. It had taken countless rebellions, wars, conspiracies, and attempts to establish 'Maroon' enclaves, before they succeeded in winning the struggle for mass liberation. In terms of Atlantic history, it was a seminal development. It was more significant historically in terms of the ideological history of liberation than the American Revolution which after all was fought and led mostly by free people. Their seizure of the colony meant the automatic abolition of the TTA. Without demand there is no market.

The greatest subversion of the TTA and the inter-colonial labour trade came with the 1805 Haitian Constitution. The leaders of Haiti, mostly the formerly enslaved, declared that any black person who arrived in the country would be declared a citizen. The legal provision effectively abolished slavery and replaced it with the conferment of citizenship and nationhood. This was the greatest revolutionary development of Atlantic modernity.

Figure 2.3

Toussaint L'Ouverture
Source: 'The Slave who defeated Napoleon' by Jennifer Brainard
http://www.historywiz.com/toussaint.htm

Enslaved blacks from all the slave systems of the Americas fled to Haiti as 'boat people' in search of liberty, freedom and citizenship. Haiti became the Atlantic beacon of black redemption and liberation — the slavers' nightmare. Boatloads arrived on its shores, fleeing from slavery, in search of the 'New World' that Europeans had found and kept for themselves. At the first opportunity available to them in the Americas, Africans had put an end to the TTA and declared it a crime. Subsequent constitutional reforms reinforced this development. The trading in Africans as enslaved peoples was abhorred by Haitians and was resisted by all means available. Haiti, then, played its part in establishing black opposition at the global level. By 1798, Toussaint L'Ouverture, revolutionary leader of St. Domingue/Haiti, and himself formerly enslaved, had surfaced as the primary anti-slaving leader of the world.

Politically, the anti-slaving process that begun in Africa had scored a major global victory over slavers and their supporters. It was success in Haiti that destroyed the largest slave market of the eighteenth century and made real the option of armed liberation in the minds of millions of Africans in the diaspora. The achievement of the black anti-slavery movement entailed a war to the finish. For them it was not only a matter of making grand philosophical and political speeches; the trade had to be stopped by all means possible.

Meanwhile, marronage — developed since the period of conquest — continued as one form of resisting enslavement in the Caribbean. In general, Maroons like Nanny of Jamaica and Chatoyer St. Vincent (see figures 2.4 and 2.5) fought for the members of their own community.

Figure 2.4 *Nanny of the Jamaican Maroons, 1700–1740'S*
Figure 2.5 *Chatoyer of St. Vincent*

Source: 'Jamaica's True Queen: Nanny of the Maroons' by Deborah Gabriel http://www.jamaicans.com/articles/primearticles/queen nanny.shtml;
Source: http://groups.msn.com/VincyPeeps/josephchatoyer.msnw

Nevertheless, Maroons resisted enslavement on a day-to-day basis and presented challenges to the planter, merchant, and colonial communities. Significant Maroon communities existed in Belize, Dominica, Jamaica, and the Guianas. Maroons led many wars against British forces in the seventeenth and eighteenth centuries resulting in several major peace treaties. The major Maroon wars in Jamaica broke out in 1730 and 1795 and were only ended by treaties in 1739 and 1796. The second Maroon War led to the deportation of many Maroons to West Africa, specifically Sierra Leone via Nova Scotia in North America.

While marronage and non-violent day-to-day acts of resistance undertaken in particular by women (described by some planters as female demons who thwarted the overseers in the field) were effective in undermining the slave system, it sometimes required outright war by the enslaved people to demonstrate their discontent and efforts to end slavery, escape from it or undermine its efficiency. Armed revolt, successful or aborted, was attempted from the early years of colonization. In Barbados, for example, there were aborted rebellions in 1649, 1675 and 1692. The sophistication of the organization and range of objectives caused the 1692 aborted rebellion to be described by contemporaries as the most complex, sophisticated and far-reaching of all. Major or minor, every sign of protest engendered a reaction from the enslavers who sought to entrench a system of control that was perceived by the enslaved to be omnipotent. The scale of executions following the suppressed attempt at protest in Barbados between 1685 and 1692 (shown in table 2.1), effectively demonstrates the power of the enslavers.

Table 2.1
Enslaved People Executed for Protesting Enslavement in Barbados, 1685–1688

Owners	Sex of the Enslaved and Number	Compensation Paid to Enslaver
James Carter	M	5,000 lbs. Sugar
Lt. Col. Helmes	2M	10,000 lbs. Sugar
Thomas Hacket	M	4,350 lbs. Sugar
Capt. Joseph Jones	M	3,000. lbs. Sugar
Arthur Nusum Jnr.	M	2,500, lbs Sugar
John Maddocks	M	5,000, lbs. Sugar
John Whetstone	F	5,000, lbs. Sugar
Daniel Richards	M	5,000 lbs. Sugar
John Reid	3M	£69
Walter Scott	M	23
John Sampson	M	23.10
Samuel Lanbert	M	20
William Andrew	M	23
Col. John Farmer	2M	8,000 lbs. Sugar
John Mills	F	£20
Capt. Burgess	2M	45
William Andrew	F	23
John Grills	M	20
Thomas Seawell	M	18
John Mills	M	25
Melatia Holder	M	25
Phillip Gamble	M	22
Susana Santon	M	22
Lt. Col. Thomas Helmes	2M	50
Charles Edgarton	M	25
Anthoney Skull	M	17.10
John Dempster	2M	34
Willoughby	1M	25

Owners	Sex of the Enslaved and Number	Compensation Paid to Enslaver
Chamberlaine	1F	15
William Wheeler	M	20
John Gibbs	M	25
Samuel Lambert	M	22
Richard Linlit	2M	2.20
Edward Jordon	M	25
William Barrow	M	25
James Walwyn	M	23
Prudence Hassell	M	18.17
John Harrison	M	2
John Evans	M	23
Zachariah Leggard	M	23.10
John Yearwood	M	22
Thomas Merrick	M	20
Ann Newton	?	13

Source: Minutes of Council 1685–1688, Reels Lucas MSS, ff. 1–540; Bridgetown Public Library, Barbados, in Hilary Beckles, *Black Rebellion in Barbados* (Bridgetown: Carib Research and Publications, 1987), 43.

Table 2.2
Sample from the List of 92 Enslaved Executed for Participating in the 1692 Protest, Barbados

Owner	No. of the Enslaved Killed	Value in £
Richard Skelton	1	25
William Bailey	1	25
Henry Nelson	1	25
Henry Applewhaite	1	25
Richard Roberts	1	25
Thomas Daywells	3	75
Ann Legg	2	50
Dorothy Earle	2	50
William Sharpe	2	50
John Peter	1	23
Thomas Estwick	1	25
Benjamin Middleton	1	25

Source: Hilary Beckles, *Black Rebellion in Barbados*, 47.

Table 2.3
Fatalities in the 1692 Protest, Barbados

Executed	92
Death as a result of castration	4
Death in prison	14
Death by miscellaneous causes including torture, illness while in weakened state, measles, et cetra	4
Total Deaths	114

Source: Compensation list: Barbados Minutes of Council, June 1694–1695, in Hilary Beckles, *Black Rebellion in Barbados*, 47.

Apart from the Haitian Revolution led first by the Jamaican Maroon Boukman Dutty and later by Toussaint L'Overture, two of the major armed wars in the eighteenth century were Tacky's (or Takyi's) War that broke out in Jamaica in 1760 and the Berbice war led by Cuffee (or Kofi). Tacky was a Ga Chief in West Africa. He was enslaved on the Frontier Estate in St. Mary's parish. There he demonstrated outstanding qualities and was made foreman of the estate. This gave him the opportunity to devise plans to gain freedom and to get those plans to his trusted fellow enslaved at Frontier and the neighbouring sugar plantations including Trinity. Before daybreak on Easter Monday 1760, Tacky and his supporters made their way to Port Maria. There they killed the shopkeeper of Fort Haldane and stole four barrels of gunpowder, 40 muskets and a supply of cannon balls. With their new ammunition, the group then went through the plantations in the area. Hundreds of enslaved people joined Tacky and other anti-slavery activists in the fight. At Ballard's Valley Estate, a few miles from Frontier, they stopped to rejoice in their success. However, one of the enslaved from the neighbouring estate, on one of the properties that had been attacked, slipped away and raised an alarm. Soon a troop of 70–80 mounted militia was on its way to suppress the war. Some sources indicate that the militia was assisted by members of the Scott's Hall Maroons who were bound by their 1739 peace treaty to aid in suppressing such wars. Other documents indicate that Tacky skillfully negotiated with the Maroons to look the other way.

By the time the whites had quelled the war several months later, an estimated 60 whites and approximately 300–400 enslaved people had been killed, including some who were tried and publicly executed as ringleaders. Another 600 were transported and sold to the logwood cutters of Belize. Oral history indicates that Tacky escaped and lived on to inspire other protest movements in St. Mary. In his bold bid for freedom, Tacky displayed the courage that made him one of the early heroes of the Jamaican and wider African diasporic peoples.

St. Mary was to be the scene of another war in 1823. While we so far have the names of Tacky, Blackwall and Quamin for 1760, there is more information on those tried and convicted by the colonial state in 1823.

Table 2.4
Partial List of Activists, St. Mary, Jamaica, 1823

Names	Sentence
Charles Brown	Hanged
Richard Cosley	Hanged
Henry Nibbs	Hanged
Morrice Henry	Hanged
William Montgomery	Hanged
James Sterling	Hanged
Charles Watson	Hanged
Rodney Wellington	Hanged

Figure 2.6
Cuffy (Kofi) of Berbice

Source: http://guyanaguide.com

The 1763 Berbice war was the other major eighteenth
century enslaved-led violent protest. While in other parts
of the Caribbean the Maroons were taking control over
parts of the colony, enslaved blacks took control of the
entire colony of Berbice. They were led by Kofi and
declared themselves the new government.

In the mid-eighteenth century, Suriname was the
largest Dutch colony with about 50,000 enslaved
Africans, most of whom worked on large sugar plantation.
There were also smaller, neighbouring colonies to the
west of Suriname — Berbice, Essequibo, and Demerara.
Berbice was a company colony that was still in the early
stages of development. The directors of the Berbice
Company were also its owners. There were only about
350 white people in the colony who were responsible for
the ownership, possession, and management of about
4,000 enslaved Africans. This means there were about
11 Africans to one European. The sugar plantations were
privately owned and the colony had about 84 plantation
owners. The directors of the company owned about a
dozen plantations.

Like many other colonies on the South American
mainland, Berbice also had about 300 enslaved
'Amerindians' (indigenous peoples). These were people
who were supposedly captured in the Dutch wars. There
were some free indigenous peoples who had either made
peace agreements with the Dutch or were licensed traders
and food suppliers. Some supported the Dutch in their
rivalry with other Europeans on the coast. Generally,
they helped the Dutch police the interior frontier, tracked
and returned enslaved runaways and worked as soldiers
in crushing black revolt. In other words, they played a
similar role to the one the Maroons of Jamaica performed
for the English after the 1739 Peace Treaty.

In February 1763, the enslaved peoples in Berbice
revolted. It was not the first time they had done so;
between 1733 and 1762 the colony had an ongoing history

of black rebellion and protests.

Like most enslaved-led wars, this one began as an action on one plantations and spread to the plantation of the other black leaders. The first plantation was Plantation Magdelenen on the Canje River. The enslaved people there killed the plantation manager and some other officers before moving on to the neighbouring La Providence Plantation. There the manager escaped but his house was destroyed, and the enslaved leaders recruited more protestors to join the war.

Within two weeks other enslaved people were at war on most Plantations on both the Canje and Berbice Rivers. Many white people were killed and taken prisoners as the activists moved from plantation to plantation. Those white people who escaped did so by fleeing down the river to coastal forts and towns, or by taking the difficult overland route to Demerara. From the end of February until early December 1763, black people had taken charge of the colony and were in command of its government.

Kofi, the mastermind behind the strategy to drive the Dutch out of Berbice, had arrived in Berbice as a young boy and was recognized on the Barkey plantation on the Berbice River on which he was enslaved, for his intelligence and good manners. As a result of these traits, he was trained in domestic service and later trained as a cooper. The Barkey plantation was at the centre of the war and due to his activism, Kofi became the governor of the colony. His second in command during the war (and later deputy governor under Kofi) was Captain Accra, also an Akan from Ghana. During the war, both took up residence in the prestigious Council House at Fort Nassau, with all the official staff and ceremony. Governor Kofi, like Toussaint L'Ouverture later, was concerned with national development. He believed that the economy should be restructured and production restarted, as trade was required to produce wealth and taxes for the government. He began to negotiate with the Dutch so as to meet these objectives. Kofi wanted to revive the plantations and produce sugar and rum for export. He wanted to become a statesman and nation-builder. Kofi was, however, like Toussaint, very clear and firm on the question of slavery, stating that it should be abolished forever.

Kofi wrote a series of letters to the defeated Governor Hoogenheim. The letters set out the anti-slavery policies of his government, and at the same time indicated a willingness to recognize the interests of the Dutch outside of Berbice. Just like Toussaint, Kofi's compromises and attempts at reconciliation with the defeated enslavers and their government representatives were his undoing. Indeed, Kofi's political understanding of the situation did not save him from the very people he recognized and described to Hoogenheim. While a letter written in May was on its way to Hoogenheim, groups within Kofi's camp were already planning further military assaults upon Daargradt, the only remaining significant Dutch settlement in Berbice. This group was led by Atta, also from Ghana. They were not prepared to negotiate with the Dutch whom they recognized as opposed to black freedom. Atta and his group were determined to drive all the Dutch out of Berbice and completely free all enslaved Africans in the colony.

So the leadership of the freedom struggle was divided — broken into two separate camps that were now at war with each other. One group declared Atta its governor, saying that Kofi was a compromiser and betrayer of the cause. June 1763 became a period of warfare between black people. Most of Kofi's men were killed because Atta had the support of the majority because he had a policy of total war against all enslavers.

Kofi was defeated but rather than fall into the hands of Atta's warriors, he shot himself in a dramatic act of suicide. It was said that his loyal followers sacrificed two

Figure 2.7
Kofi Dictates a Letter to Prins to be sent to Dutch Governor Wolfert Van Hoogenheim

Source: Alvin Thompson, *The Berbice Revolt, 1763–64* (Georgetown, Guyana: Free Press, 1999).

Europeans on his grave as a mark of respect for his leadership. Atta captured Kofi's deputy, Accra. He spared his life on condition that he worked for one of Atta's commanders. Accra subsequently escaped and surrendered himself to the Dutch. In return for his life and freedom he agreed to work for the Dutch as a spy and a soldier hunting enslaved anti-slavery activists.

In November, heavily armed Dutch troops arrived and by December 10 had defeated the activists after many bloody battles. By the end of January 1764, the Dutch had rooted out other small pockets of resistance. The revolutionaries were tried under a military court and the punishments and executions were completed at the end of June. By February 1764, one full year after Kofi's war was started the Dutch were back in full possession of the colony of Berbice. The Dutch put the remaining activist leaders to death after the Court of Criminal Justice had issued its judgements. The enslaved were defeated but many black people had enjoyed at least a period of freedom. For a year they were effective rulers of their own country.

Such defeat did not deter enslaved blacks who continued to fight for the end of the TTA and of slavery itself. The following table captures some of the major plots, rebellions and wars waged by enslaved people across the Caribbean.

Table 2.5
Summary of Resistance Movements by Enslaved People

Country	Year	Details
Antigua	1685–1700	Widespread running away and Maroons activity
	1701	Revolt by Coromantees, Greencastle estate – Christmas
	1729	Plot centred on Crump's slaves – Christmas
	1735–1736	Islandwide Afro-creole plot, led by Tackey and Tomboy
The Bahamas	1734	General slave plot revealed by Governor Fitzwilliam
	1787	Armed runaways lurking in Blue Hills, New Providence
Barbados	1649	Servile revolt reported by Ligon, possibly involving slaves as well as white servants
	1675	Coromantee plot led by Tony and Cuffee
	1683	Plot involving many enslaved Africans
	1692	Afro-creole plot, led by Ben, Sambo, and others
	1701	Afro-creole plot
Belize	1765	Revolt of Cooke's slaves from Jamaica
	1768	Revolt on New River
	1773	Revolt on Belize River – Easter
Bermuda	1656	Plot led by Black Tom and Cabilecto
	1673	Plot led by Robin and others
	1720–1731	'Poisoning Plots', including the one allegedly directed by Sara Basset
	1761	Islandwide plot led by Mingo and others
Dominica	1785–1790	First Maroon War, under leadership of Balla, Pharcell, and others
	1791	Revolt of windward slaves – New Year
	1795	Colhaut uprising, involving some slaves
	1802	'Black Man' mutiny of the Eighth West India Regiment

Grenada	1765	Slave revolt followed by widespread maroon activity
	1795–1797	Fédon's rebellion, involving majority of island's slaves.
Guyana (Berbice)	1763	Cuffee's rebellion in Dutch Berbice (preceded by slave revolts in 1733, 1749, 1752, 1762). From February to October of that year, slaves rebelled against planters. Their leader, Cuffy, an Ashanti fought valiantly but committed suicide by May of that year
	1795	Slave revolt in Dutch Demerara, in conjunction with maroons
Jamaica	1655–1670	Resistance by 'Spanish Negroes' Lubolo, de Serras, and others
	1673	Revolt of Coromantee slaves, Lobby's estate, St. Ann's parish. Approximately 300 slaves destroyed the Juan de Serras settlement in the
	1676	St. Ann's Mountain.
	1678	Revolt on Duck's estate, St Catherine's Parish
	1685	Revolt on Grey's estate, Guanaboa Vale
	1690	Revolt centred on Sutton's estate, Clarendon Parish, led by Slave revolt in Chapleton in Clarendon led by Cudjoe. Efforts of Cudjoe, the elder and the Maroons led to the signing of the 1st Maroon Peace Treaty.
	1730–1740	First Maroon War, involving Cudjoe the younger, Nanny, and many other leaders
	1742	Christmas. Coromantee plot, St. James's Parish
	1745	New Year. Plot, mainly by enslaved Africans, St. David's Parish
	1754	Crawford Town Uprising- this was a protest against harsh treatment
	1760	Takyi's (Tacky) War, dominated by Coromantee slaves, originating in St. Mary's parish at Easter, but spreading widely through island
	1765	Coromantee uprising, St. Mary's Parish, led by Blackwall
	1766	Coromantee uprising, Westmoreland Parish
	1776	Afro-creole plot, Hanover Parish, led by Sam, Charles, Caesar, and others
	1791–1792	Islandwide slave unrest after news from Haiti
	1795–1796	Second Maroon War in Trelawny and St. James's Parish
	1806	Plot in St. George's Parish
Providence	1638	Slave rebellion – Christmas

St. Kitts	1690	Slave uprising in conjunction with French invasion
	1778	Abortive Afro-creole plot – Easter
Saint Lucia	1796–1797	Brigands' War, involving many slaves
St Vincent	1769–1773	First Carib War, with Black Caribs led by Chatoyer
	1795–1796	Second Carib War, under leadership of Chatoyer and Duvallé
	1797	Kalinagos led a revolt against the British – they were defeated and were transported to the Bay Islands of Ruatan and Bonocco off the coast of Honduras.
Tobago	1770	Revolt at Courland Bay, led by Sandy
	1771	Revolt at Bloody Bay
	1774	Revolt at Queen's Bay
	1801	Afro-creole plot, centred on western half of island – Christmas
Tortola	1790	Revolt on Pickering's estates
Trinidad	1805	Plot among francophone slaves around Careenage and Maraval – Christmas

Source: Michael Craton, *Testing the Chains: Resistance to Slavery in the British West Indies* (Ithaca: Cornell University Press, 1982) 335–39.

Prior to 1807

In addition to armed resistance, enslaved Africans and their descendants protested by refusing to work or claiming that they were sick or injured. According to Barbara Bush, women played a major role in refusing to work and engaging in verbal abuse and insolence. In some cases, women went as far as to mutilate themselves. Enslaved domestics, many of whom were subjected to serial rape by their exploiters, poisoned the European enslavers, overseers, and workers, residing on their estate or plantation. Bush suggests that mothers played a role in promoting and maintaining the spirit of resistance by teaching their children from a young age to disobey the slave system.

These diverse forms of resistance so destabilized the slave regime that many planters eventually sold out and left the colonies. By 1807, Britain was forced to acknowledge that the phased abolition of slavery, starting with the trade, was inevitable. This decision was also influenced by the activism of British abolitionists — male and female — politicians and ordinary people, black and white citizens.

European and North
American Abolitionists
in Action

The eventual abolition of the Transatlantic Trade in
Africans (TTA) reqiured parliamentary intervention but
was the result of various interlocking factors. For some
historians, the Act of the British Parliament that ended
the trade was an outcome of tactical genius on the part
of humanitarians who won parliamentary and public
support. For others, however, the trade came to a logical
end under severe internal economic and external political
pressures.

European opposition to the TTA developed slowly,
and was unable to stop the march of those with an
economic interest. From the outset, there were individuals
in Europe, and among European settlers in the Americas,
who voiced their opposition to the trade. These
individuals did not build any public movements that
impacted significantly on the growth and spread of the
market in African souls. It was not until the late
eighteenth century that anything resembling a serious
political movement emerged in Europe. Even then, it
has been argued, European governments, moved to
abolish the TTA at a time that was consistent with
perceptions of their economic interests.

At the leadership level the European abolitionist
movement was dominated by the thinking of religious
groups, humanist philosophers, and a smaller category
of radical political leaders. Many were less than fully
resolved in their condemnation of the trade and most
fell short of calling for an outright, immediate abolition.
Early opposition within the Vatican was spasmodic and
had little effect. Pope Leo X was anti-TTA the TTA
rulings. His views were supported by deMercado, Bishop
of Cape Verde, who in 1569 said that slavers were morally
contaminated and guilty of a high crime.

Some clerics and philosophers were critical of the trade
in their published texts and speeches, but few were
committed to public agitation to achieve abolition.
Quakers in the English Caribbean colonies during the

seventeenth century were not opposed to the TTA or slavery in general, but called for moderation in the usage of the enslaved, and asked enslavers to cater for their mortal souls and make provisions for the freedom of those deemed good and loyal. English enslavers read this position as an attempt to subvert their full property rights in African people. The Quakers were persecuted and driven out of the Caribbean. In the mainland colonies where they settled a greater tolerance of the TTA and the slavers' world was practised by this sect. Catholics in the Spanish-American colonies were committed to trading in Africans, despite deep concerns by some of their priests. Most clerics were consistently more concerned for the enslaved native population than the Africans. They effectively lobbied the Vatican and monarchs for an abolition of trade in indigenous peoples and indigenous slavery. Whenever success was achieved in terms of a legalistic approach to improving the conditions of native Americans, it was done at the expense of enslaved Africans who were imported as substitutes. There was consensus, in fact, among church, state and settlers that the trade in enslaved Africans was the answer to the genocide associated with the enslavement of indigenous people. Catholics and Protestants alike subscribed to this new formula to develop the New World. Moral outrage at colonial slavery was confined to the question of so-called indigenous people. The leading philosopher-priest of the Catholic movement in Spanish America, Las Casas, politicized the idea from his Caribbean base that protecting the indigenous people meant trading in Africans. This, he said, was a part of the natural and divine order of things. Colonialism needed labour and enslaved Africans were the practical answer.

Queen Elizabeth I of England was sensitive to the social destruction caused by kidnapping in Africa, and urged her subjects to procure captives by 'honest' means. Kidnapping, she said, was a moral offence, but trading for enslaved people on the open market was not. Other European monarchs did not bother to engage this debate, though many, like Elizabeth, expressed opposition to the importation of Africans to Europe, as opposed to colonial society. In 1644, a New England court ordered the return to Africa of enslaved people deemed to have been kidnapped. At this time the colony was plentifully supplied with indentured labourers from the British Isles, and African slavery was not developed as an important institution. Fifty years later, enslaved Africans were dominant in the labour market, and the judicial system soon fell into line.

It is also true that many early North American colonists who objected to the TTA did so out of concern for its impact on white working-class immigration. As planters in these colonies pressed for more and cheaper labour, the supply of indentured, contract workers from Europe seemed inadequate. Yet many colonists who saw the economic benefits of using enslaved labourers feared living in a society with a black majority and idealised the option of white immigration.

Some European philosophers who spoke and wrote on the question of human liberty, social freedom, justice, and notions of the public good, supported and participated in the TTA. John Locke of England successfully established a reputation as a leading philosopher on the theory of liberty. Yet he was hardly considered compromised by the published evidence of his deep financial involvement in the TTA. Not only was Locke recognized as an authority on human liberty, he was known as a business administrator, and a principal investor in the Royal African Company, the leading English TTA corporation during the last quarter of the seventeenth century. In addition, he was an investor in the sugar plantation economy of The Bahamas. 'Locke on Liberty' was confined to the intellectual discourse;

'Locke on Slavery' was about how to make a comfortable material life.

Likewise, Thomas Hobbles provided an intellectual legitimization of slavery within his writings on freedom and the social functions of the state. He saw Africans as captives of war defeated in a power struggle by a dominant state. Their enslavement was therefore lawful and moral. Slavery for both Hobbes and Locke was consistent with modern notions of human liberty. For them it was the option to death and carried the added benefit of exposing Africans to an ascendant European civilization. The racism explicit in the work of both philosophers demonstrated the intellectual limitation of much of English liberal philosophy and provided evidence of the xenophobic aspects of European mentalities.

Effective intellectual opposition to the TTA came foremost from French Enlightenment philosophers during the mid-eighteenth century, particularly Voltaire, Charles Montesquieu, Denis Diderot and Jean-Jacques Rousseau, with stormy support from the playwriter, Pierre de Marivaux. They wrote at length about the private and public immorality of the slaving system, described its corrupting influence on civilization, and agreed that it degraded and reduced those who engaged in it as a method of earning a living.

Voltaire, in particular, rejected the anti-intellectualism of racism, specifically its white supremacy expressions, and ridiculed the idea that a so-called 'white' race was entitled to enslave a so-called 'black' race. Voltaire was persistently aggressive in his criticism of the Catholic Church, ridiculing the litany of papal bulls that endorsed the slave system and advocated the rights of whites to dominate 'others'. He regarded it a sign of ignorance that people should consider human features such as skin colour, hair texture, and facial structures important indicators of civilization, and condemned slavers as contemptible for using such arguments in justification of their trade in death.

Montesquieu, it seemed, was satisfied to focus on the argument that the slaving system brutalized the enslaver and the enslaved, both being victims of its cruelty and immorality. The slaver, he stated, loses social virtue in pursuit of economic value. The slave relationship, he insisted, was the indictment of the European within the colonial encounter. The genocide committed against the American natives, and the enslavement of Africans, he added, were driven in large part by the lust for exotic produce and the greed for gold. For him, the TTA was a harbinger of European cultural decline. How ironic, he thought, that the unsavoury business of slaving should result in the mass consumption of cheaper sugar.

Rousseau, like Voltaire, saw the TTA as the worst modern corruption of the use of economic power and political authority — both of which for him were illegitimate. The notion of a 'right' to enslave, he argued, is contradictory because the possession of 'rights' by one party and the process of enslaving another party demonstrate the illegitimate use of force. Rousseau's voice, and Voltaire's vision, combined to produce a force of intellectual opinion in France, and beyond that reinforced anti-TTA sentiment and action. Together, they showed how the Jesuit priests especially, the Society of Jesus that led Catholic missionary activities in Africa and the Americas, had lost their souls in the bid to support and benefit from colonizing agendas. By rejecting the principle that 'all men are born with a natural right to liberty', the Church, in line with John Locke's thinking, was asserting that Africans were less than human, and that only whites had such a given right.

The opposition to the TTA within the context of philosophical and theological discourse in France was strengthened by the publication in England in 1776 of Adam Smith's book, *The Wealth of Nations*. As an analysis in the political economy of capitalism, Smith's work categorized slave relations as less productive and more expensive than those found in free labour systems. At this time, in the British colonies of mainland America, the revolutionary War for Independence was demonstrating that Africans were more than keen to fight and die for the promise of liberty and citizenship. The impact of this realization on pro-slavery opinion was more than most colonists could bear. But the growing belief that the enslaved constituted a potential revolutionary army, opposed to the European colonial project, was enough in itself to generate anti-TTA sentiments and abolition movements.

When Thomas Jefferson wrote the first draft of the American Declaration of Independence, few people knew that he had fathered children with an enslaved woman, but most had accepted that the TTA had become part of the American way of life. His reference to the sacred rights to life and liberty were not meant to apply to the thousands of Africans within his private or public spaces. The Massachusetts' Assembly debated but failed to pass a resolution before the War of Independence to abolish the TTA on the ground that selling people was a violation of human rights, and more importantly that it represented the importation of rebellious material.

None of this found its way into Jefferson's legal framework for the new nation. But the everyday fear of revolutionary war by the 700,000 blacks, and the compelling discourse on human rights, combined to create a nagging political problem for the emerging nation. Both the issue of the TTA and slavery demanded discussion. In 1780, Pennsylvania advanced the anti-TTA movement by legislating that the trade was forbidden among residents from 1789, New York, New Jersey, and Rhode Island followed and so did Canada. Only the State of Georgia openly supported the slave trade.

The TTA came under increased criticism and close empirical scrutiny during the mid-eighteenth century by radical nonconformist religious groups. Baptists, Methodists and primarily Quakers spoke out against the evils of slavery in general and were key foundation members of the Society for the Abolition of the Slave Trade, formed in 1787, by Granville Sharp and his friend Thomas Clarkson. Although Sharp and Clarkson were both Anglicans, nine out of the 12 members on the committee were Quakers. Influential public figures, such as Thomas Fowell Buxton, George Fox, John Wesley, Joseph Surge, Josiah Wedgwood, Joseph Woods, James Phillips, Joseph Hooper, John Barton, Richard Phillips, George Harrison, and Samuel Hoare also gave their support to the campaign through the Society.

The group resolved that the TTA was both immoral and unjust. Buxton later campaigned for the abolition of slavery as well, and in 1823 helped form the Society for the Mitigation and Gradual Abolition of Slavery. After William Wilberforce retired from political life in 1825, Buxton became the principal public leader of the campaign in the House of Commons. Zachary Macaulay, a highly respected intellectual, supported the abolition movement. He had personal knowledge of slave trading and slavery, having been a bookkeeper in Jamaica. He found the slave system personally repugnant and campaigned for its abolition. John Wesley, a widely read author, was an influential figure in the movement. In 1774, he published a book entitled *Thoughts on Slavery*, which set out his reasons for opposing the slave trade and slavery. He thought the trade 'a scandal not only to Christianity but humanity'.

Other early attempts were made to petition parliament regarding the trade. In 1776, David Hartley presented the first Bill against the trade but this was rejected in the House of Commons. In subsequent years, three names stand out as synonymous with the movement to abolish the trade, Granville Sharpe, Thomas Clarkson and William Wilberforce.

Granville Sharp

Figure 3.1
Granville Sharp

Source: http://www.brycchancarey.com/abolition/sharp.htm

Granville Sharp was born in Durham in 1735. He became aware of the evils of the TTA when in 1765, Jonathan Strong, an enslaved black man, arrived at his home after being badly beaten by his enslaver, David Lisle. Strong told Sharp that Lisle had brought him to England from Barbados. When Lisle became dissatisfied with his work, he beat Strong with a pistol and threw him on the street. After Strong had regained his health, David Lisle attempted to recapture him. Sharp took Lisle to court claiming that as Strong was now in England he was no longer an enslaved man. The courts ruled in Strong's favour in 1768. The case received national publicity and Sharp was able to use this in his campaign against the TTA and slavery.

Even more poignant was the case of James Somerset, an enslaved man brought to England and who opposed being taken back from the Caribbean. Sharp took his case before Chief Justice Lord Mansfield who faced the dilemma of challenging property rights in enslaved people at the expense of allowing slave trading and slavery in Britain. Lord Mansfield gave his judgment on June 22, 1772, which prevented the forced return of Somerset to the Caribbean. He ruled that since there was no definite law sanctioning slavery in England it must be considered illegal. This famous case was a major victory for the anti-TTA movement.

Sharp was also involved in the case of the *Zong*, a Liverpool ship. In September 1781, *Zong* was taking 442 enslaved Africans to Jamaica. Captain Luke Collingwood lost his way and water and food supplies ran short. He reacted to the crisis by throwing 133 African captives overboard and defended his action in strict economic terms. The public outrage over the details of the case contributed to a process of re-examining moral issues involved in the TTA. Sharp was chief among those who lobbied for criminal charges to be brought against Captain Collingwood. In 1769, he published a pamphlet entitled *A representation of the Injustice and Dangerous tendency of Tolerating Slavery; or of Admitting the Least Claim of Private Property in the Persons of Men, in England*, that became a famous manifesto document for the anti-TTA movement.

Thomas Clarkson

Thomas Clarkson was born in Wisbech in 1760 and died in 1846. He was educated at St. John's College, Cambridge, and was subsequently ordained as a deacon. In 1785 Cambridge University held an essay competition and Clarkson entered his work: 'Is it right to make men slaves against their wills?' He won first place for this entry and devoted his life to abolishing the TTA.

Clarkson was instrumental in collecting scientific data to support arguments for the abolition of the trade. His investigations took him to slaving ports such as Liverpool and Bristol, where he interviewed hundreds of sailors.

Figure 3.2
Thomas Clarkson

Source: http://en.wikipedia.org/wiki/
Image:Thomas_Clarkson_by_Carl_Frederik_at_the_National_Portrait_
Galery.jpg

He obtained equipment used on the slavers such as handcuffs, leg-shackles, instruments for forcing open captives' jaws and branding irons and used them as exhibits in his public speeches. From one of his interviews, he wrote:

> The misery which the slaves endure in consequence of too close a stowage is not easy to describe. I have heard them frequently complaining of heat, and have seen them fainting, almost dying for want of water. Their situation is worse in rainy weather. We do everything for them in our power. In all the vessels in which I have sailed in the slave trade, we never covered the gratings with a tarpawling, but made a tarpawling awning over the booms, but some were still panting for breath.

In 1787 he published his famous pamphlet, *A Summary View of the Slave Trade and of the Probable Consequences of Its Abolition*, which was internationally distributed. Over 15,000 copies were circulated in 1788 alone. Clarkson

Figure 3.3
Diagram of the Slave Ship Brookes

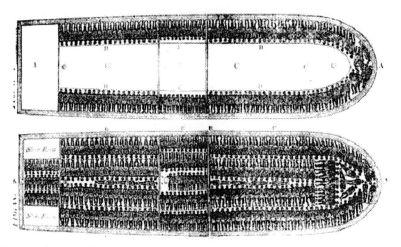

The Warðer Collection, NY
Source: Hilary Beckles and Verene Shepherd, *Liberties Lost:
Caribbean Indigenous Societies and Slave Systems* (London: Cambridge
University Press, 2004).

was also actively involved in producing images of slavers
and stressed the horrid conditions under which Africans
were transported.

This image of the *Brookes,* supplied by Clarkson,
showed men on the right, women on the left and children
in the middle. Clarkson did not focus entirely on the
danger faced by Africans in African trading, but
highlighted the impact on British families given the death
of many British sailors on slaving voyages. Mainly because
of his efforts, a Privy Council committee was formed to
look into the trade in 1788. Finally, after the passing of
the Abolition Act, Clarkson published his now classic
book, *History of the Abolition of the African Slave Trade.*

William Wilberforce

It was William Wilberforce, son of a wealthy
merchant, who led the political campaign. Born in Hull

Figure 3.4
William Wilberforce

Source: Hilary Beckles and Verene Shepherd, *Liberties Lost: Caribbean Indigenous Societies and Slave Systems* (London: Cambridge University Press, 2004)

in 1759, he attended Cambridge University and decided on a career in politics soon after graduation at the age of 20. He won a parliamentary seat for Hull and supported the Tory (Conservative Party) government led by William Pitt. In 1784 he joined the radical Clapham Sect, and became increasingly interested in social reform. Though the majority of the Tory Government was not in support of the movement to abolish the transatlantic trade in Africans, support was forthcoming from some liberal leaders such as Charles Fox, Richard Brinsley Sheridan, William Grenville and Henry Brougham.

Wilberforce argued that ending the traffic in human cargo would lead to an improvement in the Africans' living conditions. In May 1789, he made his first speech against the TTA in parliament. In subsequent debates, he argued that 'the abolition of the trade in Africans was indispensably required, not only by religion and morality, but by every principle of sound policy'. He tried to assure enslavers and traders that England's trade in manufactured goods would not suffer any setback if the trade were to be abolished, and that it would in fact increase.

When Wilberforce presented his first Bill to Parliament seeking to abolish the TTA in 1791 it was defeated by 163 votes to 88. In 1805, the House of Commons passed a Bill that made it unlawful for any British subject to transport enslaved Africans, but the measure was blocked by the House of Lords. However, with the death of William Pitt in 1806, the new Prime Minister Lord Grenville formed a 'Whig' administration,[1] which was strongly opposed to the trade. The Slave Trade Bill was passed in the House of Lords by 41 votes to 20. In the House of Commons, the bill was carried by 114 to 15 and became law on March 25, 1807.

The Society for the Abolition of the Slave Trade set up in 1783 was an exclusively male organization. Wilberforce opposed women's participation in the campaign. He was concerned that female reformers wanted to go further than the abolition of the trade. Activists such as Anne Knight and Elizabeth Heyrick were in favour of the immediate abolition of slavery, whereas Wilberforce strongly believed that the movement should concentrate on bringing an end to the trade in Africans and then gradually work for emancipation. But even though women were excluded from the leadership of the Society for the Abolition of the Slave Trade, approximately ten per cent of the financial supporters of the organization were women. In addition, Mary Birkett, Hannah More and Mary Wollstonecraft, and a considerable body of working and middle-class women in Britain were involved in the campaign from the very early stages. They spoke out against the TTA, boycotted slave-grown produce, and wrote anti-TTA tracts to raise public awareness.

The objective of abolitionists was to inform the British public of the barbarity of the TTA and its connection with sugar production. Thousands of public features and sermons accompanied the publication of hundreds of tracts with images depicting the horror of the trade. The most evocative image of the eighteenth century was a kneeling African man with the caption 'Am I not a man and a Brother'. This simple but poignant message was engraved on medallions, worn as bracelets, hair ornaments, and inlaid with gold as ornaments for snuff boxes. It was engraved on cups and other household items and contributed greatly to the awareness of the British public about the tragedy of the trade. Later the image also included a female figure and bore the caption 'Am I not a women and a sister'. (See Figure 3.6 and 3.7)

Figure 3.5
John Newton

Source: http://www.mkheritage.co.uk/cnm/htmlpages/newton1.html

The abolitionist cause won the support of John Newton a former trader. Newton was the captain of two slavers, the *Duke of Argyll* and the *African*. He was converted to Christianity in 1748 and became rector at St. Mary Woolnoth in London. In a sermon at St. Mary he stated: 'I have a conviction that the share I formerly had in the trade binds me in conscience to plead for an end to a commerce so iniquitous so destructive as the African slave trade.' He also authored the famous hymn, *Amazing Grace*, which aptly describes his conversion:

Amazing grace! How sweet the sound
That saved a wretch like me!
I once was lost, but now am found;
Was blind, but now I see.

'Twas grace that taught my heart to fear,
And grace my fears relieved;
How precious did that grace appear
The hour I first believed!

A marble plaque at St. Mary Woolnoth carried the epitaph which he wrote cementing the nature of his conversion:

JOHN NEWTON, Clerk
Once an infidel and libertine
A servant of slaves in Africa,
Was, by the rich mercy of our Lord and Saviour
JESUS CHRIST,
restored, pardoned, and appointed to preach the
Gospel which he had long laboured to destroy.
He ministered,
Near sixteen years in Olney, in Bucks,
And twenty-eight years in this Church.

Figure 3.6   Figure 3.7

Source: http://www.vam.ac.uk/images/image/22581-popup.html

Source: http://www.nationalarchives.gov.uk/pathways/blackhistory/rights/docs/am_woman.htm

Public meetings were held to enlist support and local communities were encouraged to petition parliament. For the first time, white men and women who were barely literate and who could not vote were petitioning their parliament on behalf of blacks.

Abolitionists also encouraged children not to eat sweets for the sake of balck people in the Caribbean who were enslaved to produce the sugar. Intense propaganda against the trade was a feature of the campaign. More than 312 petitions were sent into parliament from England and 187 from Scotland.

It was with this growing support that the English abolitionists introduced the 'Foreign Slave Trade Bill' in the House of Commons in 1806. Officially, British involvement in slave trading between Africa and the Americas ended the first day of 1808.

It had been a hard and bitter campaign. In the first year of the activities, Clarkson calculated the committee held 51 meetings, generally from 6:00 in the evening to about 11:00 at night and printed 26,526 reports and accounts of debates and 51,432 books and pamphlets. Abolitionists faced stiff opposition in parliament, particularly from the 'West India Party' which represented the British-colonized Caribbean enslavers.

The efforts of humanitarians and politicians coincided with economic trends within the British Caribbean economy, and British industrial transformation that enhanced the translation of anti-slave trade ideas into legislation. Trinidadian historian, the late Eric Williams argued for example, that American independence added to the success of the movements to abolish the TTA. The loss of the 13 North-American colonies diminished the number of enslaved Africans at the disposal of the British Empire and made abolition easier. In addition, he found that bankruptcies plagued West Indian sugar plantation in the years before the abolition of the trade.

Between 1799 and 1807, 65 plantations were

abandoned in Jamaica, 32 were sold for debts and in 1807, 115 had suits pending on them. The war with France at this time which led to blockades on British Caribbean produce was also contributing to the ruin of the British Caribbean planters. Williams also believed that economic pressure underpinned the abolitionists' apparently humanitarian concern. The trade was abolished, he concluded, only after parliament was persuaded that the national economy would be best served by the abolition.

Other Caribbean historians, such as Elsa Goveia, agreed with Williams. She stated,

> if the British West Indian sugar industry had not been in severe economic difficulties from the beginning of the nineteenth century, it appears most unlikely that the humanitarians could have succeeded in abolishing either the British trade in Africans or British colonial slavery.

But it is important to note, she said, that abolitionists were 'able to produce a reaction which showed that the religious and humanitarian interests in slavery had reached the critical point of no return'.

So, the British finally abolished the transatlantic trade in Africans in 1807. Parliament was persuaded that national economic and political interest would best be served by this development. The loss of the North American colonies and the existence of well-stocked Caribbean plantations meant that the economic benefits of transatlantic slaving could no longer overshadow the criminal, political, and cultural implications. In 1791, the French National Assembly had debated transatlantic slave trading and colonial slave owning, and condemned both activities. The assembly also followed the British courts (though by 20 years), in declaring that any person who arrived on French soil would be free of enslavement, but continued to distinguish between slave trading and slave ownership. In 1794, the Convention in Paris abolished slavery but slave trading continued under law.

The Danish government however declared in 1792 that from 1803 no trade in Africans would be permitted in its colonies. Their Caribbean settlements, therefore had ten years to stock up with enslaved peoples, and they did. More Africans were imported into St. Croix and St. Thomas in this time than the previous 100 years. The government was clear on the issues; the economic benefits of transatlantic slave trading had fallen to so low a level that it was not worth the moral and political criticism and outrage. The forts on the African coast, particularly Christiansborg Castle at Accra, were not profitable. Also, like the English, the Danes had shifted their labour policy from 'buying to breeding'. Colonists were encouraged to promote the natural reproduction of enslaved labourers by stimulating their fertility. In fact, it was the revised policy of all European countries that slavery could be put on a more secure and less controversial, footing, if enslavers could reduce slave mortality, especially among enslaved infants, increase birth rates, and reproduce an adequate creole labour force. It was a matter of economic rationality transcending, but responsive to moral and philosophical criticism.

Emphasis then shifted from the slaver to the slave womb as slaveowners sought to secure adequate labour supplies. Abolitionists in England, France, Denmark, Holland and elsewhere in Europe, supported this shift in policy as evidence of progress and spoke of it as an 'amelioration'.

Note

1. The Whigs were one of two political parties (or more accurately a loose grouping of people with a more liberal ideolgy than the Tories) in England and later the United Kingdom from the late seventeenth to the mid

nineteenth centuries. The Whigs' origins lay in constitutional monarchism and opposition to absolutism. Around 1784, Charles James Fox became the leader of a 'Whig' party, while William Pitt led the 'Tories'. The Whigs were originally also known as the 'Country Party' (as opposed to the Tories, the 'Court Party'). By the first half of the nineteenth century, the Whigs came to encompass not only the supremacy of parliament over the monarch and support for free markets and free trade, but also the abolition of slavery and democratic reform.

Freedom Delayed:
The Trade in Africans
after 1807

Between the 1807 abolition of the Transatlantic Trade in Africans (TTA) and the 1833 emancipation legislation, the transfer of enslaved people from one colony to another was represented as an extension of the TTA. Its expansion was encouraged by enslavers but was anathema to abolitionists.

The collapse of St. Domingue, the region's largest sugar producer, following the 1790s anti-slavery revolution and the emergence from its political ruins of the independent state of Haiti there in 1804 was a seminal moment. It opened up the sugar market to new producers and stimulated greater demand for enslaved people's labour in newly acquired colonies such as Trinidad and Demerara.

Primarily for financial reasons, the abolition of the TTA was welcomed by some planters in the smaller traditional colonies, most notably Barbados. The fear in these territories of competition from sugar producers in larger colonies, particularly those acquired during the imperial rivalries in the era of abolitionism, was real enough. But abolition was dreaded in Jamaica and indeed in all the large colonies. Planters who invested in agriculture other than sugar were quickest to resign themselves to a gradual demise. This range of attitudes and positions fuelled regional and imperial politics and provided much of the evidence and arguments used on both sides of the debate.

The pattern and volume of intercolonial trading in Africans were determined by the level of demand across the region and were reflected in economic and demographic trends. Net exporters tended to be the smaller colonies where the sugar sector was in decline or where attempts at the diversification of the economy were in crisis. Net importers were generally the larger sugar colonies. The trend was movement away from the smaller sugar economies and non-sugar sectors. Barbados and the Leeward Islands (St. Kitts, Antigua, Nevis, and

Montserrat), where soils were exhausted and labour productivity was low, as well as the Windward Islands (Grenada, Dominica, Saint Lucia, and St. Vincent), where the non-sugar sector had gained ground, supplied slave labour to the frontier colonies of Trinidad and Guiana (Demerara and Essequibo in particular).

The Windward Islands, ceded from France to Britain after the Seven Years War in 1763, constituted a primary net exporter. They were part of a wider trend, including The Bahamas that saw the movement of enslaved people away from the non-sugar sector — coffee, cotton, cattle, and towns — toward the sugar sector. This movement took place between and within colonies such as Jamaica. Although the Jamaican sugar sector was a significant market for slaves from The Bahamas, it also attracted enslaved people from other parts of the rural economy as well as from the urban and domestic sectors.

In addition, net-importing colonies were generally those with enslaved populations that were experiencing systematic natural decline on account of relatively greater mortality rates. They were least likely to have population structures conducive to natural growth. Neither were slave management policies directed at the enslaved supportive of reproduction. Trinidad, for example, possessed more arable acreage than all the smaller colonies combined. According to Wilberforce, it required a million enslaved workers, over the course of 100 years, in order to maximize its sugar-producing capacity.

Wilberforce's estimate was based on the observation that Jamaica, with a comparable amount of prime sugar lands, had imported at least a million enslaved people under British rule since 1655 but had less than half that number when the trade was abolished. The new colonies had a mere 105,000 enslaved people between them (Demerara and Essequibo had 80,000, and Trinidad 25,000) in 1807 and were restricted to importing fewer than 4,000 per year — less than 30 per cent of the rate in

1806, when the Act was passed.

As was the case elsewhere in the region, export (mainly sugarcane) agriculture was the reason for Britain's considerable interest in Trinidad. Not surprisingly, according to Meredith John,

> in 1808, there were 3,680 urban and 18,303 enslaved plantation workers in Trinidad. Enslaved plantation workers constituted 83% of the total enslaved population. In 1811, there were 3,891 urban enslaved people and 17,397 enslaved plantation workers in Trinidad, so plantation slaves constituted 82% of the total enslaved population.

Plantations produced mostly sugar. John noted that of the 17,087 enslaved plantation labourers on the island in 1813, 12,256 worked on plantations that grew sugar as their sole commercial crop; 1,146 enslaved people tended coffee, 1,104 grew cocoa, 779 produced foodstuff and 506 cultivated cotton.

The settlement of Demerara in 1803 during the war with the French availed the English of sugar lands greater than those on offer in Trinidad and Jamaica. Demerara had the lowest per capita enslaved population and the second highest negative growth performance among the enslaved population. This development caused considerable anxiety within the anti-slavery camp. It was believed that the two new colonies would stimulate renewed confidence in the slave economy and spiral demand for enslaved labourers.

Furthermore, legislators who supported the abolition agenda — no matter how it was conceived — understood that the expansion of the sugar frontier could endanger much of what was done by way of ameliorating the conditions of enslaved people. In general, they feared that the enormous injection of fresh acreage into the plantation economy would relegate emancipation considerations to the bottom of imperial concerns for at least 50 years. It was for this reason that the Pitt government in seeking to keep faith with Wilberforce, agreed in 1805, two years before the seminal legislation, to limit the ability of these colonies to acquire enslaved Africans.

The influential Barbadian sugar producers were divided. They had within their ranks a minority who saw a brighter future in migrating to the new colonies. But most saw the new spaces as presenting competition in the years ahead and wished them closed. Barbados alone was experiencing sustainable growth among the enslaved population in 1807. The colony furthermore had been a steady exporter of enslaved people for at least two decades — mostly to the Windward Islands — where merchants and planters had been making important capital investments.

In this regard Barbados established a reputation for being 'overstocked' with enslaved people and was expected in some quarters to supply its needy neighbours. But while colonists there were looking for new opportunities in neighbouring frontier colonies, they were also keen to protect the competitive standing of what they had already created. The impact of the 1807 legislation varied considerably within and between colonies. Abolition subverted the enormous economic capacity of Trinidad and the Guianas. Neither surpassed Jamaica as a large-scale sugar producer. Jamaica was weakened but was expected to survive by introducing labour management measures in order to increase both production and productivity.

Uneven economic conditions were reflected in the price and productivity differentials between net-exporting and net-importing colonies. This circumstance contributed principally to the general direction and volume of transfers of enslaved people; and the Windwards and the Leewards were among the first to admit that their soils were exhausted by sugar monoculture and that the proximity of abundant fertile soil was a major attraction. Planters in the Windward Islands in particular did not feel confident in post-1807 conditions and many folded up their operations and looked to sell enslaved workers in Trinidad.

As part of the campaign to attract new investments from the older colonies as well as from Europe, sugar producers in the Guianas and Trinidad highlighted their advantage in labour productivity, which they measured in tonnage of sugar output per enslaved. Although they also emphasized superior sugar yield per acre, the focus was on labour because this was the scarce factor of production. By drawing attention to low prices for enslaved workers in the older colonies and showing considerably higher prices in their economies, they hoped to sponsor a significant transfer business.

Settlers in Demerara also boasted such advantages over colleagues in Berbice which had been a major Dutch sugar colony during the eighteenth century. Significant inflows from Berbice contributed to the absolute growth in the enslaved population after 1807. The colony also benefited as a result of transfers from the islands, some coming from as far away as The Bahamas. The relative increase was greater in Demerara, a reflection of the widespread expectation that the sugar sector would yield much greater profits than could reasonably be imagined in the islands.

Relative to earlier periods, the number of enslaved people transferred between colonies after 1807 was substantial, although in no way was it comparable to the annual input from the TTA. In the decade before 1807, the sugar colonies landed large number of enslaved Africans from Africa. Even The Bahamas, which was not a sugar colony, was a major importer, although a significant share of the enslaved were re-exported. Jamaica was heavily dependent on the African market, as were the new colonies of Trinidad and Guiana.

According to Philip Curtin, Trinidad imported 12,400 Africans in the years between 1797 (the year of its attachment by the British) and 1807. Barry Higman considers Curtin's figure a significant underestimation of the numbers. He noted that at least 9,000 were imported from Africa in the years 1802, 1803, and 1805. Furthermore, he asserted that the vast majority of the enslaved in the newer colonies on the eve of the 1807 abolition were recent African imports.

After 1807, these newer colonies continued to experience rising demand for enslaved labourers that could only be legally met by intercolonial trading. Williams deduces from the fragmented evidence that at least 13,000 enslaved Africans were imported into the Guianas and Trinidad between 1808 and and that most of these came from Barbados and the Windward Islands. He emphasizes the inability of the data to yield an accurate count but draws attention to the increasing numbers over time and the lack of political will within colonial administrations to clamp down on expansion.

Higman concludes that about 20,000 enslaved people were transferred to the newer colonies during the period and suggests that although the figure was considerable in the context of policy and legislative actions against trading in enslaved people, it was not large enough to have a transformative impact on general demographic and economic trends within the regional slave system.

Transfers of enslaved people were never sufficiently large to act as a stabilizing or reversing factor in the negative growth performance of net-importing colonies. At no stage did the aggregate number of enslaved Africans transferred exceed five per cent of the total enslaved population in any of these colonies. Neither did a colony export more than ten per cent of its enslaved population during the period. According to Eltis,

In the busiest single year, 1816, less than 0.5% of the
enslaved population was involved. In Berbice, the
Bahamas, and Dominica, none of which had very large
numbers of enslaved people, exports were never more
than five percent of the enslaved population in the
twenty-two-year period.

Less is known about the profiles of transferees but
there is enough evidence to show that their impact on
the demographics was negligible in terms of general trends
and patterns.

Eltis also acknowledges the limitations of the data.
He concludes nonetheless that 'more than 22,000 slaves
were shipped between the various British Caribbean
colonies in the twenty-three years after the abolition of
the African Slave Trade.' Only three colonies had net
imports on a significant scale. These three — Demerara,
Trinidad and St. Vincent — attracted imports from all
across the Caribbean, but in each case there were one or
two colonies which supplied the vast majority of the
imports. Demerara drew heavily from Berbice and less
heavily from The Bahamas and Dominica; Trinidad's main
sources were Grenada and Dominica and to a lesser
extent Barbados; St. Vincent's inflow came largely from
Dominica and The Bahamas. Custom House records for
Trinidad show double-digit import levels for the years
1813–16 coming from 12 colonies.

Significantly, neither Williams nor Eltis includes in
their calculations the thousands of 'liberated Africans',
people captured on the seas from illegal slavers by the
British Navy and employed as apprentices in labour-
starved colonies. Neither has there been an attempt to
estimate the number of captives who were smuggled
between colonies. Yet widespread allegations of extensive
smuggling should indicate that it might have been larger
in volume than legal transfers. Most colonies reported
cases of smuggling from colonies across as well as within

imperial lines.

Governors frequently reported cases in which local officials were in sympathy with sugar planters and condoned the breach of law. Lowell Ragatz concludes that in most cases 'sensational allegations' of rampant smuggling, when investigated, 'appear to have been barren of results'. Williams however suggests that the payment of one guinea per head to the chief custom officer for each captive forfeited was part of an attempt by the governor to suppress the illegal activity that might have been running ahead of legitimate commerce.

Several laws were passed by the British Parliament in order to reduce and control the movement of those enslaved between colonies. The result was a network of interconnected laws passed over the course of two decades. The 1806 'Act to Prevent the Importation of Slaves' focused directly on enslaved people supplied from Africa. It did not outlaw the movement of enslaved people between colonies but established a licencing arrangement that monitored and restricted such transfers.

In this way parliament made provision for local adjustments to the secondary labour market by identifying a number of special circumstances under which transfers would be exempted. A licence was to be acquired from the local government in order to take an enslaved person out of the colony, and the enslaver was required to post a bond for the captive named. In order to facilitate the normal migrations of free people between colonies, legislators exempted free people who carried up to two Africans provided that they were household servants, sailors, or fishermen, and their names registered with the captain as passengers.

An additional provision was made to further burden individuals who wished to transfer captives into Trinidad and Demerara. A licence also had to be acquired from the governor of the importing colonies. Furthermore, a limit was placed on the ability of these colonies to accommodate incoming Africans. A ceiling was set to contain the annual inflow at no more than three per hundred of the existing enslaved population. This meant that a governor was expected to constantly review the changing demographics of the enslaved population in order to effectively implement the policy.

Williams makes much of the evidence that suggests how imperial policy was conceived to encourage subversion of the law by means of the compliance and corruption of local officials. He stresses that legislators were not concerned unduly with this aspect of the TTA. Knowing the difficult and awkward positions governors generally occupied in these colonies, he implies that legislators might have established the machinery with the expectation that breaches would be defended locally.

Eltis states the case in different terms. He focuses on an imperial tendency to develop policy more for the protection of British capital than to enhance the well-being of the enslaved population. A major concern was that post-war negotiations would lead to the return of these colonies to their former imperial owners. By the signing of the post-war treaty Trinidad and Demerara were ceded to Britain. This outcome removed doubts about the future of capital investments and facilitated the expansion process.

The 1806 Act was not intended to stem the flow of enslaved peoples between colonies. What alarmed those who lobbied against the TTA was evidence showing that the smuggling of captives into these colonies was also done with the support of local officials. Shutting down the Atlantic trade was the top priority for British legislators, but this objective made it necessary to push another Bill through parliament in 1811 making the illegal trade in enslaved Africans a felony.

It is possible that more Africans were smuggled across imperial lines than were legally transferred between colonies. But neither the 1807 Act nor the 1811 Act developed serious penalties to combat the continuous expansion of the inter-colonial trade in enslaved Africans. Slavers argued that such laws would not be acceptable and that the imperial government could not break their resolve to reject restrictions on the enjoyment of their property rights in enslaved Africans. Cases of smuggling were prosecuted under the 1806 and 1811 laws but were generally met with political responses and solutions that indicated the difficulties faced by the colonial judiciary in suppressing both types of trafficking in enslaved Africans.

Unable to stem the illegal flow in enslaved Africans and bring order to the transfer trade, abolitionists argued that enslavers were doing all they could to subvert the law and as a result adopted a two-part strategy. First, they suggested that a head count approach to the problem was the only reliable way to identify illegal imports and monitor the legitimacy of legal transfers. This required colonies to develop census materials in order to register the enslaved population in a way that would enable significant demographic changes to be identified.

James Stephen, heading the campaign for the Colonial Office, called for a comprehensive, centrally organized registration system as early as 1812. By means of an Order in-Council, the governor of Trinidad partially instituted such a system. According to Ragatz,

> Census returns for 1812 had shown an official total of 21,288 slaves in the colony; the first registration of 1813, four and a half thousand more — 25,717. This increase was seized upon . . . as proof that extensive smuggling had taken place and became the basis for a four year long struggle to establish compulsory registration in all the Caribbean possessions.

Enslavers disagreed with Stephen's conclusion and used public institutions as sites of opposition. They foregrounded the argument that the required registration of all captives was part of the abolitionists' plan to push through a bill for general emancipation. This argument posed a special political problem for the Barbadian enslavers who had used it to explain the large-scale war that erupted among their enslaved workers in April 1816.

In their opinion, the anti-slavery activits had acted in support of the abolitionists who had secured the support of the monarch for general emancipation. The blacks in turn had articulated the view that their protest was an attempt to implement the royal wish as expressed by abolitionists. Enslavers, in defending their interests, were providing ideological ammunition to those enslaved for their emancipation campaign.

The second approach was to gradually reduce the size of legal transfers by further narrowing the band of select categories. This meant new legislation because previous Acts were considered too generous. Two separate acts passed in 1818 and 1825 sought to address this concern by targeting occupational groups who could be legally transferred rather than imposing numerical limits. These laws provided that only enslaved domestics, sailors, and fishermen could be exempted from the licencing arrangement.

At the same time the 1818 Act relaxed the provision that new colonies could import annually under license from old colonies a number of enslaved people up to three per cent of the existing enslaved population. The argument used by legislators was that the removal of the cap was in the interest of the captives. Such transfer, the Act stated, might tend to ameliorate the material condition of the enslaved in economically depressed colonies. This adjustment reflected slaveowners' reasoning that in the crisis-ridden non-sugar sector in colonies such as The Bahamas and Dominica, those enslaved were experiencing severe hardship, and only their removal to more prosperous areas could prevent catastrophic disaster.

The 1825 Consolidated Slave Act with which the imperial government legally declared its policy of gradual emancipation, formally tied applications for enslaved people to the Amelioration project. The focus shifted away from occupational groups and limits to the nature of the impact of relocations on the captives. According to the terms of the Act only the British Privy Council could issue import licences, and it was expected to do so only on the submission of evidence that the captive would benefit. Furthermore, the law obliged enslavers to provide a bond as evidence of commitment to keep families intact and that the enslaved would travel in relative comfort.

The enslaved community held views regarding transfers that were articulated with much the same passion and precision as those of the free community. There was no single, simple opinion among its members, who could be grouped into three broad categories. First, some among the enslaved were assertive proponents of amelioration policies and resisted attempts to restructure and disrupt their social lives by relocation. They were keen to report objections to magistrates when family members were slated for relocation and often confronted owners in large groups when told of transfer proposals. Estate and court records, for example, reflect the link between the social instability associated with transfers to frontier colonies and marronage. The enslaved knew as well as whites that Trinidad and Demerara were experiencing considerably higher mortality rates and were notorious as places where the work regime was harsh as well as deadly. Soggy, waterlogged valleys, plains, and swamplands, were being drained and prepared for sugar cultivation. The enslaved knew of the debilitating work this project entailed. Their health experiences and medical culture had taught them to avoid areas such as these which were infested with mosquitoes.

Second, those enslaved understood the hardships

related to subsistence in some colonies, particularly in the Windward Islands. Part of the push from these colonies was the crisis of subsistence that produced among some enslaved a keen material interest in relocation. Flight from hardship, therefore, was not confined to whites. Furthermore, there were instances in which enslavers and enslaved agreed to approach resettlement jointly with enthusiasm.

The third category included the enslaved who were a part of the normal clandestine movement between colonies. They knew the physical landscape and general living conditions across the region in as much detail as did members of the free community. Island-hopping labourers, including fugitives from the law, had established a survival network that operated between colonies. The knowledge they gained was shared with the enslaved community and was a feature of its social and political life.

The flexible aspect of slave relations in these colonies enhanced mechanisms whereby the enslaved were allowed to 'freely' travel between colonies looking for work or selling goods. Barbadian hucksters and enslaved artisans, for example, who were 'self employed' and who paid a part of their income to owners, were keen travellers between colonies in search of better wages and price while the enslaved held a range of opinions regarding resettlement. In general, the evidence suggests that the majority held reservations about it and were likely to protest relocation.

Abolitionists in the British government would instruct governors to enforce the law by ensuring that voyages made between colonies to transfer the enslaved in no way resembled the Atlantic crossing. This meant that the enslaved were to be treated as passengers rather than cargo. The assurance, however, could not be given. With the opening of frontier colonies, slave owners began the practice of using the transfer mechanism as a form of punishment for rebellious or insubordinate enslaved peoples. Part of the punishment was shipment in chains.

Being sold 'overseas' during this period was a part of the reign of terror that enslavers considered an effective strategy. Such concerns informed the decision of Parliament to outlaw after 1828 all transfers except for fishermen, sailors, and domestics accompanying their owners. But critically, there continued to be no obligation for owners to take these enslaved people when they returned to their homes.

After 1828 a greater onus was placed on people wishing to transfer an enslaved worker to show evidence of ownership or legitimate possession, residency in the colony from which the person was being removed, that the enslaved was attached as a servant companion of the person in whose name the licence was issued, and that the two were to travel on the same vessel. This approach proved equally open to abuse. According to Williams, an interesting question arose as to whether infants, much in demand, could properly be considered domestics within the meaning of the Act.

For all practical purposes the 1828 regulation was ineffective. The evidence from Trinidad and Demerara indicates that there was widespread violation of its provisions. Customs officers seemed quite amused, notes Williams by the arrival of a stream of 'domestics' ostensibly in the employ of ladies and strangers. Many of these blacks were sold to people willing to take the risk of travelling with them, while those who could not attract buyers were left behind.

Williams's conclusion that the degree of fraud was large is borne out by the descriptions presented to the Colonial Office by governors. With respect to Barbados, Governor Lyon was satisfied that many enslaved people taken to Trinidad were not kept in the domestic service of people they accompanied but were bound for resale or conversion to plantation labour. In his judgment, there was little more that could be done to stop this movement, described by a colonial official as 'an unfeeling traffic', so long as the enslaver could obtain twice or three times the price by selling the enslaved in frontier colonies.

Not surprisingly, Demerara and Trinidad became net importers in the decade between 1818 and 1828. Higman shows that the former achieved a net import balance of 7,500 between 1808 and 1828 and the latter secured a net import balance of about 6,000 between 1813 and 1825. The principal net exporters were The Bahamas, Berbice, Barbados, and Dominica. Net importing colonies did not report satisfaction that the labour shortage was impacted, and there continued to be a feeling in the exporting colonies that there was insufficient work to productively employ the enslaved labour force.

The number of enslaved people transferred to the newer colonies, was insufficient to alter in any meaningful way the principal demographic features of any one colony. Enslavers were unable to control the composition by age and sex of transfers. Certainly, they would have preferred to import a predominately male labour force for the development of plantation infrastructure. Lacking selective control for age and sex, enslavers did not consider the transfer business efficient and they much preferred the range of choice available within the Atlantic trade before 1807.

Trinidad's statistics for the peak period of 1815–25 show the ineffectiveness of transfers with regard to these factors. For a sample of 538 enslaved people transferred from The Bahamas to the colony in 1822, the ratio of males to females was 107:100. For The Bahamas at the time of export the sex ratio was 104:100. Furthermore, with respect to the 2,500 enslaved people imported into Trinidad between 1822 and 1825, there were 115 males to 100 females. Higman concludes from these data that although the enslavers were able to attract a relatively large number of men from the older colonies they did less well than when they had participated in the Atlantic trade.

An important reason for insufficient cohort control was that most of those transferred into Trinidad came from a few large plantation properties and from the urban sector in exporter colonies. It was the norm for entire groups of enslaved workers to be transferred from a given plantation with no regard to gender or age differences. In the case of Barbados, the majority of enslaved workers transferred between 1817 and 1820 originated in Bridgetown, the capital, and its environs. After 1825, when mainly domestics were exported, the parish of St. Michael, which hosted Bridgetown, was a principal exporter of the larger female component.

James Stephen was keen to show that such transfers were not directed at the expansion of the sugar sector — as argued by investors in frontier development — but was an aspect of the legacy of mercantile speculation associated with slave trading. His findings regarding illegal transfers were presented to the government as part of an effort to show the importance and wisdom of a compulsory registration policy. He relied on informed people in the colonies to supply the data that he shared with parliament.

In 1828, Stephen told the government:

> There appears very strong grounds for suspecting that the great comparative value of the enslaved in Trinidad has tempted many persons to make fraudulent importations from Barbados, by attributing the character of domestic enslaved people whom it was never intended really to employ in that capacity.

Data for Trinidad show that of 266 enslaved people who were imported from Barbados under licence in 1827, 204 were no longer in the employ of the person in whose name the licence was issued. Another group of 81 were doing jobs that fell outside the category of 'domestic'.

Enslavers and their legal representatives contested as best they could efforts by the imperial government to impose such restrictions on their right to use their chattel in a manner beneficial to themselves. They objected to being defined as legal offenders by imperial officials who assumed that each change of a worker's occupation was done in an attempt to subvert the law. Rising to their defence, Attorney General Henry Fuller of Trinidad told enslavers that no law existed in the colony to prevent their redeployment of enslaved people from domestic service to field gangs. Many domestics, he said, preferred life on the plantation to life in the towns, and many did not consider the seasonal nature of field work more burdensome than house work.

Similarly, a customs official in Barbados, disputing the governor's claim that the trade in domestics to Trinidad was in fact a covert traffic in field hands, argued that were the numbers large the Africans themselves would have objected. In 1829, the controller of customs, while objecting to this allegation, reminded the governor that the enslaved in Trinidad and Guiana, unlike their counterparts on the island, were invested with the power to appeal to the Protector of Slaves, a public official who survived the changeover from Spanish to English law. On being informed of such a facility, a Colonial Office spokesman replied that local enslaved domestics would carry the greater burden since they would be sent to the fields in order to make room for imported domestics.

In Barbados, the 1829 Franklin case gained notoriety throughout the region because it symbolized slaveowners' views concerning the use of legislation to control and limit the intercolonial transfers. For Williams, the case indicated the lengths to which enslavers went in opposition to anti-slavery policy and imperial officials in the colonies. On the surface the case began like many others. Franklin, described in the records as a modest enslaver, received various licences in order to ship 14 of the enslaved to Trinidad. He indicated that they were to travel with his family. These individuals, most of them children, were not put to domestic work and as a result Franklin was adjudged to have violated the law — an offence for which he was imprisoned.

The trial by grand jury predictably led to Franklin's acquittal. His peers took the view that enslavers should not be presumed to be criminals for altering the nature of their workers' occupation. Empowered by the verdict, Franklin secured substantial funding to bring a suit against the magistrate who signed the documents under whose terms he was sent to prison. Significant sections of the colonial elite, many lawyers included, rallied to his aid in seeking damages to the value of £5,000 (colonial currency) for false imprisonment.

News of the case reached neighbouring colonies and was widely reported in the press. Franklin was described by the governor as a 'man of straw' who was backed by men of substance whose interest it was to create a 'system of intimidation' and 'embarrass the Government' in order to compromise and repress the 'efforts of public officials . . . in the prosecution of offenders'. The Colonial Office understood all too well that Franklin was in charge in name only, and that the struggle 'had really been waged with the Officers of Customs rather than with him'.

The battle, though, was much wider in scope. The field of contest was the very future of British slavery in the Caribbean. Imperial interests were still in a celebratory mode with respect to the bounty represented by two large frontier colonies. Some enslavers in the 'old' colonies were anxious to take the new breath of life offered by large tracts of fertile soil. The frontier had obvious economic attraction for investors. The collusion of imperial and colonial interests in this regard seemed sufficiently compelling to allow the market to deter-mine the outcome.

Abolitionists however had other ideas. They saw the

potential in these colonies for a grand revival of interest in colonial slavery and used the practice of intercolonial transfers of enslaved people to test the durability and depth of their support in the British legislature. They were determined to limit the ambitions of slavers who saw in the frontier colonies a new lease on life. The old colonies, they knew, ran the risk of dying on the vine unless they could wean themselves from any kind of African trading, and the new colonies would not be allowed to take a case for rolling back the abolitionist policy.

The enslaved too had their say in determining the outcome of the debate and the formulation of ameliorative legislation. They knew the limitations of their political voice but in general turned their faces against the new colonies until slavery was abolished. The point was not lost on enslavers that the post-1807 movements of enslaved people were taking place within a charged political environment that featured not only imperial rivalry but an upsurge in the number and frequency of protests in the aftermath of the Haitian anti-slavery war.

Barbados, considered the 'safest' of England's colonies on account of not having experienced a major protest in the 'long' eighteenth century, had its first enslaved-led war in 1816. Demerara followed in 1823, and reports of the connection between these wars informed popular understanding of intercolonial linkages between the enslaved. Both wars were associated, at least in the of the enslaved mind, with the idea that registration procedures were a prelude to emancipation.

This was the enslavers' own line, and they had been hooked by their enslaved workers. When slavery was finally abolished, blacks in Barbados migrated by the thousands to Guiana and Trinidad in search of new opportunities for self-empowerment. The colonial government was forced to pass anti-migration legislation to stem the tide for fear of having the local labour force decimated.

The internal Caribbean trade in enslaved peoples then, raised more ideological issues in political fora than it resolved economic problems on the frontier. Abolitionists may have had their finest hour in effectively marginalizing the new frontier within the empire. They ensured that the expansionist possibilities of newly acquired colonies did not rise on the basis of an emerging slave system in the way that was the case in Cuba at the same time. For this important reason it would not be accurate to say that the intense debate and the many legislative interventions were much ado about nothing.

Legacies: Persistent Racism and New African Identities

It is estimated that over 100 million people of African ancestry now populate diaspora communities in Europe and the Americas. Their everyday experiences continue to be adversely affected by forces released during the slavery period. Changes and continuities in the black contemporary experience should therefore be set out and examined against this background.

By the end of the eighteenth century three aspects of the Transatlantic Trade in Africans (TTA) were universally known:

- Transatlantic trading in Africans had become a way of life within the Atlantic world. There was popular agreement in Europe, and among European settlers in America that the TTA, and black slavery, were necessary for the advancement of New World colonialism, and European global interests.

- The critique of the TTA on moral, political, or economic grounds was a separate issue from the wider question of maintaining slavery, and ought to be treated differently in discussions about Europe's relationship to Africa and African peoples. In this regard, most people in Europe who were prepared to publicly oppose the trade in Africans were not willing to reject slavery as an institution or African colonialism in general.

- Most Europeans of all classes were aware of some benefits which they derived from the TTA, particularly its role in the economic development of Europe and the widespread belief in their social, economic and military superiority over Africans. This value system was understood generally as an important part of Europe's cultural heritage.

Such developments meant that attempts to stop the TTA would encounter considerable opposition, not only from people with a direct material interest, but from a wide cross-section of civil society. The passage of abolition legislation in Europe meant that people representing the popular opinion that enabled the trade to proliferate for nearly 400 years had to be re-educated. It was understood by anti-slavery advocates and organizations that the battle for real abolition and emancipation would have to be fought in the years ahead in the hearts and minds of white society.

The politics of anti-slaving, anti-slavery, and anti-racism were considered separate issues. Some advocates were prepared to oppose the kidnapping of Africans, their shipment under the horrid conditions of the Middle Passage but cared little for the perceived negative effects upon African identity and society. Many such individuals remained in support of slavery and racism on economic, political and social grounds after emancipation. Racism, remained a powerful ideology and took on new expressions into the twentieth century.

The political debates over the abolition of the TTA — which divided Europe and colonial societies — opened to academic scrutiny the spread and depth of anti-African racist opinion within white communities. The pro-TTA argument was based on a series of propositions and opinions which were held to be true. Widespread belief in the notion of black inferiority found expression in the many texts and oral statements. The intensity of 'negrophobic' commentaries revealed the extent to which some whites had come to see civic society in terms of hierarchical racial structures. The anti-TTA movements did not have as a principal objective an ideological confrontation with anti-black racist attitudes and opinions; many white abolitionists subscribed to the views of the pro-TTA trade group that blacks were culturally inferior and would benefit from long-term tutelage within

European civilization. While they agreed that it was the white man's burden to civilize black people, they were merely opposed to slavery as the mechanism. The TTA, in their opinion, was an inappropriate and illegitimate instrument for the implementation of the agreed objective.

TTA abolitionists found it necessary to support the continuation of slavery. While for some this was a tactical move in order to win broad based political support at the parliamentary level, for many it was the end of the line as the evil was not in slavery itself, but in the trade — the kidnapping, wrecking of West African society and econom, and the evils of the Middle Passage.

Europeans added other twists to the tale. They were more keen to abolish slavery at home before they gave any serious consideration to its ending in the colonies. The English case was typical. The legal judgement of Lord Mansfield in the 'Somerset Case' of 1771 says a great deal about the thinking that had matured within the context of the abolitionist movement. Judge Mansfield ruled that English law did not recognize slavery in England, and that English society was free of the vile relations of slavery. All blacks in England were to be freed because the English, at home, considered themselves too advanced a people 'to breathe the foul air of slavery'. English law abolished slavery in England in 1771, but kept the TTA to its colonies until 1807, and maintained colonial slavery until 1838. Other European societies presented similar political and legal paradoxes; what was not acceptable at home was satisfactory for the far-flung colonies. These time frames and conceptions of space within abolitionism presented it as a tortured and torn process. Also, they help to explain the persistence of institutional racism against African people long after the end of the TTA and the abolition of slavery. It is necessary however to say something about the colonial emancipation process in order to gain insights regarding the survival of negrophobia after the slaving system was dismantled. In all colonial slave systems, with the exception of Haiti, the emancipation process was not designed to economically empower or socially liberate the black people. Emancipation was planned and implemented by colonial and imperial legislators to ensure the continuation of white, economic, political, and social domination. Blacks were to continue as social subordinates trapped within institutional systems that assured their second-class status within society. In fact, when the concepts of citizenship and nationhood were debated, blacks were excluded generally on racial grounds by white political leaders. For them the ideal emancipated African was a wage labourer or share-cropper who functioned as a politically disenfranchized individual who accepted social marginalization.

Imperial governments and their colonial administrations, held clearly this vision of 'free' society. 'White over black' was the agreed upon political formula; only blacks and a few radical supporters sought to destabilize this model by active resistance and rebellion. In the United States of America, for example, an attempt was made to offer some compensation to blacks by granting a mule and land, but again the thinking here was how best to ensure a pool of resident, cheap, labour for white farmers to continue their economic accumulation. In the case of the British in the Caribbean this much was clear. Enslavers received as a subvention from the imperial government the sum of £20,000,000. This sum was granted as compensation for the loss of their property rights in blacks following the passage of the Emancipation Act of 1833. Substantial financial support to enslavers was also intended to empower them to strengthen their hold over the colonial world in the aftermath of emancipation. In effect, it meant an investment in the future of the white elite — planters and merchants — in order for them to perform the tasks of social management in the new dispensation. The blacks received no compensation.

The United States of America fought a war of national liberation but kept slavery as the organizing principle of social development. This tainted the moral and political importance of the revolution. Furthermore, the contradiction of building a new nation committed to liberty and freedom upon the foundation of slavery exploded and sent its citizens back to the battlefield to fight one of modernity's bloodiest civil wars in search of resolution. But the Civil War, while bringing about black emancipation, also stimulated the growth of an enormous amount of anti-black racism that hovered on the edge of genocidal actions and attitudes.

The inability of post-slavery societies to embrace blacks as citizens with equal civil rights particularly in the new nation states of North and South America was reflected in the enduring legacies of race hatred that only centuries of racialized chattel slavery could bring. In Latin America, blacks were subjected to similar kinds of community attacks as in the USA. Violent, white supremacy organizations, such as the Klu Klux Klan, routinely killed and persecuted blacks and others committed to realizing the full vision of liberty offered by emancipation legislation. The criminal lynching of blacks became a past time of such groups in the USA. Emancipation, ushered in an assiduous war against blacks by racists throughout the Americas.

At the centre of the nineteenth-century emancipation discourse was the experience of Haiti — the land, according to an English anthropologist, where 'black rules white'. The Africans in Haiti had done what whites had always feared even though every conceivable precaution had been taken. They revolted, destroyed the slave system, took control of their destiny, and declared the liberty of African people as an act of self-actualization. It was the first and only time in the colonial world that blacks had liberated themselves and taken political control of an entire society. They did this in a long and destructive war that resulted in the unilateral declaration of national independence. This was not only a major event in the European colonial project, it was the first time in human history that enslaved people had destroyed a slave system, declared themselves rulers, and maintained that status in the face of open international hostility. The Haitians did this at a time when the entire hemisphere remained engulfed in slavery. They were the first in the modern period to declare the complete, simultaneous, abolition of African trading and slavery, and the universal right of man to be free of enslavement.

The European imperial system went on the counter-attack. France tried its utmost to regain its 'colony' and engaged in negotiation with the English and Spanish governments to secure black re-enslavement. Napoleon's troops were soundly defeated by the Haitians long before the English demolished them at the Battle of Waterloo in 1815. As an international drama in the Caribbean, the Haitians took credit for first subverting Napoleon's grand imperial design.

Haiti came to symbolize all that the European imperial world resented. France refused to recognize its 1804 Declaration of Independence. So too did the English, Dutch, Germans, Portuguese, Spanish, Swedish, Norwegians, Danish and the Americans. They all took the view that French recognition was a prerequisite to official recognition and the French were demanding compensation for the loss of their property — human and inanimate. The Haitians refused to comply for some 21 years but finally capitulated in 1825 under the weight of unprecedented international diplomatic pressure. The terms of the settlement that Haiti made with the French government in 1825 was that France would recognize the independent state in return for compensation fixed at 150 million gold francs. For over another 100 years the Haitian government paid this indemnity. It bled the national treasury, and assigned the economy to endemic impoverishment. Throughout the nineteenth century there were periods when up to 60 per cent of public revenues was paid to France contributing to the chronic political instability and underdevelopment of the economy. In addition to this considerable financial burden, the European and American commercial worlds continued to treat the Haitians as outcasts in the world economy.

The racial denigration of emancipated blacks was linked in nineteenth-century colonial discourse to a process referred to as the 'Haitian menace'. Racist intellectuals in Europe especially, who had been pro-slavery in their thinking, explained the economic and political instability of Haiti in terms of black incompetence and inferiority. Thomas Carlyle, the noted nineteenth-century English political philosopher, wrote a number of essays on what he termed 'The Nigger Question' in which hostile popular sentiments about blacks were expressed. Freedom for blacks, he argued, was a tragic mistake bred in the minds of misguided and naive liberal politicians who had failed in their duty to help the 'primitives' by keeping them to tutelage through slavery.

Carlyle's racism found considerable support from a wide range of prominent European and American intellectuals. Academics, particularly anthropologists and so-called natural scientists, produced a virtual revolution in publications dedicated to proving the mental and moral inferiority of blacks. In the twentieth century, literary outpouring from some of the most prestigious universities and publicly influential philosophers, supported this thesis from several disciplinary angles. They examined the anatomies of blacks, compared them to monkeys and apes, and advanced a spectacular number of hypotheses that now constitute what is called 'scientific racism'. Freed from slavery, entrapped within white supremacy systems— economic, legal and political — blacks were now the target of a major intellectual effort to demonstrate, within the methods of the social and natural sciences, that they were mentally inferior to whites. The objectives of this racist intellectual work were four fold:

1) to rationalize and justify black enslavement and African colonialism
2) to explain human development in its material and social aspects in terms of concepts of race and colours
3) to promote social policy that calls for the physical segregation of 'races' and 'colours' in community planning
4) to effectively stereotype blacks as the principal antisocial criminal element within white society

In European societies, public political debate called for policies to keep black immigration to a minimum as an effective strategy to obstruct any movement towards multiracialism as a conceptual framework for social development. In the Caribbean and Latin America blacks remained politically disenfranchized into the mid-twentieth century, and subjected to race-based socio-economic exclusion. The alleged social 'whitening' of Latin America as public policy surfaced as a direct post-slavery response. Institutional racism everywhere was the principal strategic response of former slave owners to public governance.

These developments were supported by events that transformed Europe's relationship with Africa. Following the abolition of slavery came the so-called 'scramble' for Africa. Success in the acceleration of military assaults on Africa by Europe in the last quarter of the nineteenth century was symbolized by the fall of Ashanti. After 400 years of human resource extraction in the form of the TTA, Europe was now politically empowered to exploit all other African resources. This colonialization process popularized and expanded the evidence available to advocates of white supremacy thinking. The imperial domination of Africa in the wake of emancipationism nullified the validity of opinions that had promoted abolitionism as directed by an upsurge of popular political goodwill towards Africans. Rather, it confirmed the view that the slave trade and slavery had outlived their usefulness to Europe, and that more effective methods of plundering Africa's resources were desired. Eric Williams's argument that the slave system had become anachronistic in the age of matured industrial capitalism remains compelling for the reason that Western industrialism now desired control over productive resources other than labour.

European settler societies in Africa, were designed to demonstrate the modern thinking about blacks. The Dutch, French, Portuguese, and English respectively, established racially segregated communities in Africa based on the concept of political exclusion. These societies evolved into what became known as the Apartheid regimes of South Africa and Rhodesia (now Zimbabwe). Similar communities were also established in East Africa and South West Africa. Apartheid upgraded the principle of black oppression and exclusion that had typified the slave system. Variations of the social concept were found at the same time in the USA, the Caribbean and Latin America.

The process of black resistance however did not cease. The forms it has taken have been modified to meet changed circumstances. The commitment of blacks to freedom and justice remains endemic to the wider Atlantic world. By the 1920s the evidence of this posture throughout the African continent and the Americas was found in a proliferation of organizations and movements committed to black advancement. The issues of citizenship, nationhood, national sovereignty, human, and civil rights, generally embraced the thinking of these groups and individuals.

In the years following World War II, the objectives of blacks in Africa and its diasporas were being clearly articulated by their own leaders in international fora — particularly the United Nations. A number of issues were taken by them to centre stage in the international community. They included:

1) preparations in Africa for the building of mass movements with the objective of decolonization and winning national independence
2) establishment in mainland American diasporas of civil rights organizations dedicated to the attainment of racial justice and equality
3) the rise of labour movements and political parties in the Caribbean that sought the attainment of full civil rights for all, and the ending of colonialism in the form of the establishment of independent nation states

These combined processes represented the considerable energy and consensus on development which existed among blacks. During the 1930s and 1940s, Africa and its diasporas forged important operational, intellectual, political, and cultural links with the objective of advancing the decolonization process. The Marcus Garvey movement provided a major organizational and intellectual framework that reached across the Atlantic. The attempt by the Ethiopians to hold out against Italian military pressures focused attention on the need for a strong Pan-African sensibility. The re-emergence of Ghana in 1957, independent of British colonialism, was a major step forward. Diaspora community leaders had played major roles in Ghana's liberation. Prominent among these were George Padmore and C.L.R. James, both from Trinidad, and William Du Bois from the USA, all of whom are now enshrined in the annals of Ghanaan sovereignty.

Following Ghana, political developments in Africa included the attainment of national independence by most African countries — some of which were forced, as they did in the slave period, to pay the greatest costs in the forms of the mass loss of human life. The final collapse of apartheid in Southern Africa during the 1980s and 1990s signalled in many ways the ending of another era in black freedom in Africa and elsewhere. In many parts of the Caribbean it is important to note that the descendants of slaves now occupy the highest political offices in societies that have been radically transformed by the struggle for freedom and justice. The movement from 'slave' to 'prime minister', and 'president' for example, that had typified Haiti in the early nineteenth century, has become the common realty in most of the Caribbean at the beginning of the third millennium. In most of these countries the celebration of 'Emancipation Day' as an official public holiday speaks to the political importance attached to the meaning and significance of the uprooting of slavery. While these societies continue to battle with the adverse legacies of the slavery experience, the idealization of the 'up from slavery' concept in public life indicates that there is a strong opinion that the process of emancipation is not complete.

In the Caribbean, Latin America, Europe, and the USA, blacks remain economically marginalized and oppressed, even though forms of political democracy and social openness have been established. The ownership structure of economic resources and access to institutions in the financial networks continue to show ethnic patterns that indicate black marginalization. The continuing criminalization of black males in many socities, and evidence that black communities are targeted in violent crimes in Europe and Brazil, for example, remain a reality of the black experience a century after the dismantlement of the slave system.

Despite these and other such international hostilities and challenges, blacks in Africa, and its diasporas, continue to pursue relentlessly their own advancement by making important contributions to the development of humanity. The cultural space we now call the 'West', for example, is in great part, a creation built by the considerable contribution of African peoples. The effective exploitation of their labour power, scientific and technological know-how, irrepressible demand for freedom, liberty, and justice, and the relentless expressions of all-embracing cultural and philosophical world views, have shaped and textured an Atlantic world that came into being as the site of Western modernity. In the achievements of this modernity, however, Africans have paid a high price, hence their continued contestations and desires to secure for postmodernity a stronger will to reject all notions of slavery as strategies for human developmental progress.

Conclusion

The process of ending the British Transatlantic Trade in Africans was politically acrimonious, socially divisive, and drawn-out. In 1788, the British founded a 'Committee for Effecting the Abolition of Slave Trade', led by Thomas Clarkson. The society agreed on a two phased approach, separating the campaign to abolish the TTA from general emancipation.

Meanwhile, in the Caribbean, the enslaved community had moved further along with respect to its own course of abolition action. A successful war led by the enslaved community in the French colony of St. Domingue in 1791, placed it firmly in the political hands of chief military commander, Toussaint L'Ouverture who immediately moved to abolish the TTA and slavery. In 1804, the blacks unilaterally declared their independence from France, and in a certain way, from Britain also. Britain had made an ill-fated military attempt to capture the colony from L'Ouverture.

The Haitian state, confronting the slave-owning powers of Europe and the USA, proclaimed abolition politics the centre of its domestic and foreign policy at the outset, consistent with the ten year anti-slavery revolutionary war from which it emerged. It was the first nation of its kind in the modern world, an inspiring expression of the endemic abolition movement that had long typified the Caribbean colonial experience. The British parliament passed its legislation to abolish the TTA on March 25, 1807 to become law in May 1807.

The abolition of the British TTA has traditionally been presented as a benevolent act by the British state that acquiesced under the mounting pressure of opposing intellectual voices and the mass advocacy of religious and humanitarian activists. There is substantial literature that details this rich history but as this text has shown it does not give adequate attention to the political role of enslaved communities in the Caribbean, who in the context of the wider Atlantic dimensions of the TTA, were its fiercest foes.

Enslaved blacks everywhere focused their resistance politics upon both aspects of the crime against humanity — the TTA and slavery itself. The Haitian constitution, for example, reflected the precise thinking of the majority of the enslaved in the Caribbean. By providing that any enslaved person who arrived in Haiti would automatically become free and a citizen, it set a benchmark in abolitionist politics for all nations. This legal facility was the most significant abolitionist development in the wider Atlantic world. By the time of the British Act in 1807, L'Ouverture's revolutionary vision and policy had been operative for over a decade, gaining for him the status as principal abolitionist leader in the Caribbean, the Atlantic and beyond. Enslaved people from near and far were already fleeing to freedom in St. Domingue before the state of Haiti was declared.

The interactions between Caribbean and European abolitionists have not been fully researched and certainly not recognized. Pride of place in the global abolition campaign has gone to the ideological and political leadership of the British, and to a lesser extent, the French. The British led the most persistent parliamentary campaign. But they also made the most money from the trade. The Portuguese may have shipped more enslaved Africans across the Atlantic but the British extracted the greatest per capita profits. This commercial circumstance had much to do with the timing and intensity of the British campaign.

The British abolitionist campaign had a significant impact upon the Caribbean movement. First, there was King William IV going public in support of the TTA; then there was the tragedy of *Zong;* and finally the Wilberforce song that confirmed black Caribbean perceptions of the British movement.

British-produced news about the TTA, like Caribbean generated rumours of black rebellion, traversed the

Atlantic at hurricane speed. The enslaved in the islands had a saying, derived from an ancestral proverb, that 'if you wish the truth to be known, you must tell it to the winds'. The *Zong* was another line in the silent tune the enslaved whispered to the wind. Ships would arrive. The news was always bad. With the *Zong* the mortality number told was 133, more or less; with other ships it might have been more or less, 20 or 30. Numbers could not measure the magnitude of grief when it was the sight of ships carrying chained souls for sale on bloody shore that was the cause of pain. The event, however, led to a Parliamentary debate that signalled the onset of professional persistence in the national campaign.

Sections of the British public rose in moral indignation at the news of mass murder on the high seas by one of their subjects. For thousands of the enslaved in the Caribbean the tragedy broke the silence surrounding the frequency of Middle Passage massacres. It certainly helped in consolidating a popular perception of the Atlantic Ocean as a mass burial site within the black community. Many had witnessed or heard of similar murders as a result of captivity on the West African coast, and in the 'passage'.

Blacks knew that in the financial world of slavers ocean deaths were rationalized as inevitable collateral damage. Ferguson notes that the 'narratives that followed on the heels of the *Zong* murders took place in the Caribbean and promoted rebellion'. How closely knitted relations of these events were remain to be known, but the *Zong* case did serve to indicate the distance between enslaved communities and the British public with respect to knowledge and emotional reactions to the TTA.

British abolitionists were not as single minded as their Caribbean counterparts. They were part of a wider movement dedicated to forging an agenda for domestic political reform. For some, the TTA was an expression of what had gone wrong with public governance, and opposition to it was expected to serve as a moral barometer and political catalyst. The enslaved in the Caribbean focused on the singular importance of opposition to the slave system, of which the TTA was a part. While the enslaved heard much about the campaign in Britain and observed closely the reactions of the white community around them, they had no reason to consider that it would bring them any meaningful solace or security.

The enslaved broke conceptually with British abolitionists on matters of family. During the eighteenth century, eminent white male abolitionists did not centre the devastating impact of the TTA and enslavement upon African family life. This came later. Africans however had moved to the fore in rejecting the legal definition imposed on them by enslavers as domestically demeaned, socially uprooted and therefore perfectly mobile chattel.

Females within the campaign did formulate opposition to the TTA in the area of domesticity that resonated with the African experience. Hannah More's poem, 'Slavery', for example, represented a link to the heartbeat of black abolitionist writers such as Olaudah Equiano, who described the pain of being torn from his family, his sister especially. She wrote:

> See the dire victim torn from social life, The shrieking babe, the agonizing wife! She, wretch forlorn! Is dragg'd by hostile hands, To distant tyrants sold, in distant lands!... By felons hands, by one relentless stroke, see the fond links of feeling Nature broke! The fibres twisting round a parent's heart, Torn from their grasp, and bleeding as they part...

Even in the finest writings of female abolitionists Ferguson shows the racial arrogance and contempt for Africans, considered dependent inferiors, tinged the ideological itinerary of the campaign. Black writers, public speakers, and campaign advocates despite their important contributions to the British movement did not escape the net that was cast over the entire race. Ferguson notes,

> Put in terms of realpolitik, the garnering of some cultural power for British white women was won at the expense of African material reality because the closer the country came to an abolitionist politic, the more imperative writers found it to denote racial difference.

Phillis Wheatley, Ignatius Sancho, Equiano, and Ottabah Cugoana would have understood this all too well as it coloured the social relations they encountered daily.

Each time an enslaved person escaped captivity, it constituted a strike against the supply side of the production system, which in turn triggered the demand side of the TTA, hence the notion of the entrapment of the African. But the intention of escapees to return to Africa speaks to the depth of the resolve that sustained black abolitionism. Mullins describes the case of an arrivant who ran away from an estate and was believed to be in Kingston, Jamaica, looking for the ship that brought him from Africa. It was his intention to board the ship for what he hoped would be its return voyage to Africa. The data on runaways in Kingston show that many were sustained by 'shipmate' ties. Shipmate support systems describe the case of 'two Ibos, a Coromantee, and a Congolese', who attempted 'to leave Jamaica in a canoe', and of 'five Bonny Country men and a Congolese who went to sea in a twenty-four foot canoe' in efforts to return home.

In general, black advocates within the British campaign did not endorse the racist ideology of black dependency, symbolized by the iconic 'trademark' that showed a black male and female on their knees beseeching compassion from whites and affirmative action. This was not comparable with their own journey to freedom and use of an independent anti-slavery voice that entailed considerable personal enterprise, self-motivation and energetic interpersonal networking. As a consequence, Midgley concludes, 'black resister' was 'integrated into the British anti-slavery movement', and in other ways, 'remained very much an outsider'.

When the Act was eventually passed, it was weakened by politically inspired compromises, gutted of its purest intent, and lacking the sharp, clinical edge of Toussaint's instrument. The enslaved community, more than any other, understood the social implications of its provisions. An inter-Caribbean slave trade, described as transfers, flourished in the aftermath of the abolition of the TTA as slave owners and slave traders devised means, some legal and others not, to move the enslaved between colonies.

Families continued to be shattered as people were placed on transfer lists and shipped out to other colonies. Slavers captured on the high seas by British patrols spewed out 'liberated' Africans in the terrifying death hole that was Demerara. Jamaican enslavers, shocked by the stoppage out of Africa, began the process of driving domestic and skilled workers into field gangs, destabilizing the enslaved community's sense of itself as a relatively ordered place. There was some celebration in order to show exuberance in the face of the enslavers' sense of their defeat. But it was not full emancipation but 'full free' which was not a part of Wilberforce's agenda. The enslaved knew, finally, that the Wilberforce song was in fact a war song, and that it was time to reinvigorate their struggle and to 'tek force wid force'.

Appendices

APPENDIX 1

THE ORDER-IN-COUNCIL OF 1806

Overview

The Order-in-Council mandating the end of the trade to the Crown Colonies was passed on August 15, 1805. Present was "The King's Most Excellent Majesty in 'Council'. On the advice of the Privy Council, the King ordered that

from and after the first Day of December next [1806], or upon the Publication of a Proclamation to that Effect within each Colony, it shall not be lawful, except by special Licence as hereinafter mentioned, for any Slave or Slaves to be landed upon any of the Coasts, or imported or brought into any of the Ports, Harbours, Creeks, or Roads or within the Limits, Jurisdictions, and Territories of any of the Settlements, Islands, Colonies, or Plantations on the Continent of America, or in the West Indies, which have been surrendered to His Majesty's Arms during the present (Napoleonic) War, until further Order, upon Pain that all Slaves so landed, imported, or brought, contrary to the true Intent and Meaning of this Order, together with the Vessels bringing in the same, or from which the same shall be landed, and their Cargoes shall become forfeited to His Majesty, His Heirs, and Successors.

The curious thing was that some trading was still allowed. The Order stated that

whereas it may be expedient to permit the annual Introduction of a limited number of Slaves, under due Regulations, for the purpose of supplying any waste that shall take place in the Population on particular

Estates, from extraordinary or unavoidable causes, and thereby of keeping up the cultivation of the Lands already cleared and cultivated; It is therefore ordered that any number of Slaves, not exceeding Three for every Hundred of the whole number of Slaves in the said Settlements, Islands, Colonies, and Plantations respectively, (Returns of the Number whereof shall be made from Time to Time, in Pursuance of Instructions to be transmitted by One of Our Principal Secretaries of State,) may be imported in each year, (provided casualties to that Extent shall appear to have taken place in the preceding year) under Licences to be previously granted by the Governor, Lieutenant Governor, or Officer administering the Government of the said Settlements, Islands, Colonies, and Plantations, from any other of His Majesty's Colonies in the West Indies, into the said Settlements, Islands, Colonies, and Plantations, respectively; such Licence, or a Copy thereof, to be produced by the Master of the Ship on which such Slaves are laden, as his authority for having slaves on board destined to the Settlements etc., as aforesaid Provided always, that, until the First Day of January, One thousand eight hundred and seven, such limited Importation may be made from other Places than His Majesty's Colonies in the West Indies as aforesaid, and without its being necessary for the Master of the vessel, if such with at Sea, to produce the said Licence, or a Copy thereof, as his authority for having the said Slaves, destined as aforesaid on board; but subject, nevertheless, to such Licence being first had and obtained as aforesaid before any Slaves shall be permitted to be landed or sold from such vessel in any of the said Settlements.

Still, the numbers allowed were small and the phased abolition of the TTA had begun.

Summary of Clauses

1. As of 1st December 1806, it shall be illegal, except by a special licence, for any Africans to be landed in the 'ceded territories'.
2. If the regulation set out in 1 is broken, the Africans and the vessel transporting them shall be seized and forfeited to His Majesty, His heirs and successors.
3. But some estates may need to import Africans to replace those who have died in order to keep up cultivation. Such estates can secure a special licence to allow for such limited importation of Africans.
4. The number to be imported annually by those to whom the special licence is granted should not exceed 3:100 enslaved peoples in the total population of that property.
5. Licences are to be produced on demand.
6. Regulations not should affect those Africans who are crew members or household servants of officials or passengers.
7. Ships carrying more than the allotted numbers allowed to be landed by special licences shall be forfeited.
8. Ships forced to land in British colonies because of damage or bad weather shall be allowed to land their slaves, as long as those slaves shall eventually be exported to non-British colonies; and they can only remain for 10 days before being required to be exported. On the other hand, such Africans could be sold to those planters qualified to buy them under the terms of the special licence allowed.
9. One-third of every forfeiture which shall accrue to His Majesty, etc. shall be granted to the Officer administering the government of the colony and one-third to the party who facilitated the prosecution.
10. The Customs Office is to keep a close watch on the sale of Africans in the ceded Colonies.

At the Court at Weymouth
the 15th Day of August 1805

Present
The King's Most Excellent Majesty
in Council

It is this Day ordered by His Majesty, with the advice of His Privy Council, that from and after the first Day of December next [1806], or upon the Publication of a Proclamation to that Effect within each Colony, it shall not be lawful, except by special Licence as hereinafter mentioned, for any Slave or Slaves to be landed upon any of the Coasts, or imported or brought into any of the Ports, Harbours, Creeks, or Roads or within the Limits, Jurisdictions, and Territories of any of the Settlements, Islands, Colonies, or Plantations on the Continent of America, or in the West Indies, which have been surrendered to His Majesty's Arms during the present War, until further Order, upon Pain that all Slaves so landed, imported, or brought, contrary to the true Intent and Meaning of this Order, together with the Vessels bringing in the same, or from which the same shall be landed, and their Cargoes shall become forfeited to His Majesty, His Heirs, and Successors: But whereas it may be expedient to permit the annual Introduction of a limited number of Slaves, under due Regulations, for the purpose of supplying any waste that shall take place in the Population on particular Estates, from extraordinary or unavoidable causes, and thereby of keeping up the cultivation of the Lands already cleared and cultivated; It is therefore ordered that any number of Slaves, not exceeding Three for every Hundred of the whole number of Slaves in the said Settlements, Islands, Colonies, and Plantations respectively, (Returns of the Number whereof shall be made from Time to Time, in Pursuance of Instructions to be transmitted by One of Our Principal Secretaries of State,) may be imported in each year, (provided casualties to that Extent shall appear to have taken place in the preceding year) under Licences to be previously granted by the Governor, Lieutenant Governor, or Officer administering the Government of the said Settlements, Islands, Colonies, and Plantations, from any other of His Majesty's Colonies in the West Indies, into the said Settlements, Islands, Colonies, and Plantations, respectively; such Licence, or a Copy thereof, to be produced by the Master of the Ship on which such Slaves are laden, as his authority for having slaves on board destined to the Settlements etc., as aforesaid Provided always, that, until the First Day of January, One thousand eight hundred and seven, such limited Importation may be made from other Places than His Majesty's Colonies in the West Indies as aforesaid, and without it being necessary for the Master of the vessel, if such with at Sea, to produce the said Licence, or a Copy thereof, as his authority for having the said Slaves, destined as aforesaid on board; but subject, nevertheless, to such Licence being first had and obtained as aforesaid before any Slaves shall be permitted to be landed or sold from such vessel in any of the said Settlements: And whereas special Instructions will be immediately transmitted by One of His Majesty's Principal Secretaries of State to the Governors, Lieutenant Governors, or Officers administering the Government of the said Colonies, Settlements, and Plantations respectively, containing the Regulations proper for carrying this Order into effectual Execution, directing and empowering them to grant Licences for the Importation of such limited numbers of Slaves as aforesaid, subject to such Regulations as in the said Instructions will be provided: It is His Majesty's further Order that such Governor, Lieutenant Governor or other Officer as aforesaid, shall be, and they are hereby respectively authorized and empowered to grant such Licences, upon such Terms and Conditions, and subject to such Regulations, as in Conformity to, and in Furtherance of, the object of such Instructions, may from Time to Time, be required; and it is hereby further ordered, that the Prohibition herein before contained shall not extend to prevent the importing and landing of any Slaves which shall be imported into the said Colonies, Islands, and Plantations by Licence first had for importing the same, under the Hand and Seal of His Majesty's Governor or Lieutenant Governor or Officer administering the Government of the Colony, Settlement or Plantation, into which such Slaves are to be imported, specifying the Ship or Vessel permitted to import the same, in Conformity with the Instructions to be received from One of His Majesty's Principal Secretaries of State as aforesaid, but that all Slaves, except such Slaves as may form Part of the Crew of any Vessels, or may be Household Servants to the Passengers therein, which shall be landed without such Licence as aforesaid and without conforming to such Regulations as shall be contained therein, shall, together with the Vessels bringing the same, or from which the same shall be landed, and their Cargoes, become forfeited to His Majesty, His Heirs, and Successors.

And in case any Vessel shall contain more Slaves than the number permitted to be imported in such Vessel, by any such Licence or Licences such Number of the most valuable of the Slaves on board such Vessel, (other than such Slaves as may form Part of the Crew of such Vessel, or may be Household Servants to the Passengers) as shall be equal to the Excess beyond the Number mentioned in such Licence or Licences, shall be forfeited to His Majesty, His Heirs, and Successors and shall be selected and disposed of in such Manner as may be in that Behalf directed by any Instructions from One of His Majesty's Principal Secretaries of State, to be given to the respective Governors, Lieutenant Governors, or other Officer administering the Government of such Colonies,

Settlements, and Plantations as aforesaid. And it is hereby further ordered and provided, that nothing herein contained shall be extended, or construed to extend, to the landing, importing, or bringing in of any Slave or Slaves from or by any Vessel which by Stress of Weather, or by any other Peril, shall be driven on the coast of any such Colony, Settlement, or Plantation, or compelled to take Refuge on such Coast, or within the Creeks and Harbours of such Colonies, Settlements, or Plantations, provided the Slave or Slaves which shall be so imported, landed, or brought in, as last aforesaid, shall be exported to some Place or Places other than any of the Colonies, Settlements, or Plantations to which this Order applies, within Ten days from the Importation, landing, or bringing in of the same, unless further detained by the Stress of Weather; or provided the same shall, within such Ten days, be sold under the special Licence of the Governor, Lieutenant Governor, or Officer administering the Government of the Colony, Settlement, or Plantation, where such Slaves may be, to such Person or Persons as, under the circumstances of his, her, or their Cases, (which circumstances shall be inserted in such special Licence) may, at the Date hereof, be entitled to obtain a Licence or Licences to import such Number of Slaves as he, she, or they shall, in and by such special Licence or Licences, be permitted to purchase, and the Right Honourable Viscount Castlereagh, One of His Majesty's Principal Secretaries of State, shall give all necessary Directions herein accordingly.

And it is hereby further Ordered and declared, that one Third of every forfeiture which shall accrue, in consequence of this Order, to His Majesty, His Heirs, and Successors, shall be granted to the Governor, Lieutenant Governor, or Officer administering the Government of the Colony, and one Third to the Party who shall inform and prosecute for the same.

And it is hereby further Ordered, that all Sales of

Slaves, imported after Notice being published to that effect by the Officer administering the Government of the Colony, shall be made publicly in the Presence of some Officer of the Customs, and the returns thereof shall be kept according to the Regulations which shall be prescribed for that Purpose in pursuance of the Directions to be transmitted for that purpose by Viscount Castlereagh, as above mentioned: And the Right Honourable the Lords Commissioner of His Majesty's Treasury are to give the necessary Directions herein accordingly.

(signed) Steph:Cottrell

Copy of the Order-in-Council, August 15, 1805, for prohibiting the Import of Slaves.

Delivered by the Earl Spencer, pursuant to an address to His Majesty – Title read – and copy ordered to lie on the Table, May 16, 1806.

APPENDIX 2

THE 1807 ABOLITION ACT

Overview

The decision taken on March 25, 1807 by the British Parliament was that as of May 1, 1807, the trade in Africans conducted by the British should be abolished. No ships should be outfitted from British ports to sail to Africa. Trading of captives from West Africa between British ships and foreign countries was also outlawed; so was the transshipment of enslaved people from British possessions to other slave colonies and the insurance of ships involved in the trade. Ships that had been cleared to participate in the TTA before May 1, 1807 and that would arrive by March 1, 1808 were exempted. Those who contravened these regulations had their ships and 'cargo' seized, or they were fined; but it will be noticed from a close reading of the various clauses of the Act that for every fined imposed, 'one moiety' — that is 50 per cent — was sent to Britain 'for the use of His Majesty, His Heirs and Successors' The British government therefore still found a way to profit from the illegal slave trade. Other clauses of the Act stipulated that if anyone liberated slaves he would receive £40 for a man, £30 for a woman and £10 for every child under the age of 14. The captives seized from illegal slavers were deemed 'Liberated Africans'; but many found themselves back on the plantations as enslaved people rather than back in Africa as free people.

Summary of Clauses

1. From May 1, 1807, the TTA shall be abolished. Penalty for trading in or purchasing Africans, &c. £100 for each African.

Le Roy le Veult

Whereas the ... ... Two Houses of Parliament did by their Resolutions of the tenth and Twenty fourth day of June One thousand eight hundred and six severally avow that they ... ... would with all practicable expedition take effectual Measures for the ... Abolition of the African Slave Trade in such Manner and at such period as might be deemed advisable **And whereas** it is ... ... fit upon all and each of the Grounds mentioned in the said Resolutions ... ... that the same should be forthwith abolished and prohibited and declared to be unlawful Be it therefore **Enacted** by the King's Most Excellent Majesty by and with the advice and consent of the Lords Spiritual and Temporal and Commons in this present Parliament Assembled and by the authority of the same ... That from and after the first day of May One thousand eight hundred and seven the African Slave Trade

MS page of the 1807 Abolition Act

2. Vessels fitted out in the UK or the colonies, etc. for carrying on the TTA shall be seized and owner prosecuted.

3. Persons prohibited from removing and enslaving inhabitants of Africa, the West Indies, or America, from one place to another, or being concerned in receiving them &c. Fine of £100 for infringement of this regulation.

4. Vessels employed in such removal, &c. to be forfeited, as also the property in the enslaved persons.

5. Insurances on transactions concerning the TTA not lawful. Penalty £100 and treble the amount of the premium.

6. Act not to affect the trading in Africans, exported from Africa in ships cleared on or before May 1, 1807, and landed in the West Indies by March 1, 1808, &c.

7. How silver taken as prize of war, or seized as forfeitures to be disposed of.

8. Bounty to be paid for such Africans to the captors in the way 'Head Money' is paid so the sums shall not exceed the rates mentioned in the Act.

9. Certificates to be produced to entitle to bounty.

10. Doubts of claim to bounty to be determined by the Judge of Admiralty.

11. On condemnation of forfeitures of enslaved for offences against this Act, the rates herein mentioned shall be paid, &c.

12. Counterfeiting certificates felony.

13. How penalties and forfeitures to be recovered and applied.

14. Seizures may be made by officers of customs or excise, &c.

15. Offences to be inquired of as if committed in Middlesex.

16. His Majesty may make regulations for disposal of Africans after the expiration of their apprenticeship.
17. Africans enlisted in His Majesty's forces not entitled to the benefits of limited service, &c.
18. General issue may be pleaded.

ANNO QUADRAGEISIMO SEPTIMO
(In the 47th year)
GEORGII III. REGIS
(Of King George the 3rd)

CAP. XXXVI. /CHAPTER 26

An Act for the Abolition of the Slave Trade. (25th March 1807)

1.   Whereas the Two Houses of Parliament did, by their Resolutions of the tenth and Twenty-fourth days of June One Thousand eight hundred and six, severally resolve, upon certain Grounds therein mentioned, that they would, with all practicable Expedition, take effectual Measures for the Abolition of the *African* Slave Trade in such Manner, and at such Period as might be deemed advisable And whereas it is fit upon all and each of the Grounds mentioned in the said Resolutions, that the same should be forthwith abolished and prohibited, and declared to be unlawful; be it therefore enacted by the King's most Excellent Majesty, by and with the Advice and Consent of the Lords Spiritual and Temporal, and Commons, in this present Parliament assembled, and by the Authority of the same, That from and after the First Day of May One thousand eight hundred and seven,

the *African* Slave Trade, and all manner of dealing and trading in the Purchase, Sale, Barter, or Transfer of Slaves, or of Persons intended to be sold, transferred, used, or dealt with as Slaves, practiced or carried on, in, at, to or from any Part of the Coast or Countries of *Africa*, shall be, and the same is hereby utterly abolished, prohibited, and declared to be unlawful; and also that all and all manner of dealing, either by way of Purchase, Sale, Barter, or Transfer, or by means of any other Contract or Agreement whatever, relating to any Slaves, or to any Persons being removed or transported either immediately or by Trans-shipment at Sea or otherwise, directly or indirectly from *Africa* or from any island, Country, Territory, or Place whatever, in the *West Indies*, or in any part of *America*, not being in the Dominion, Possession, or Occupation of His Majesty, to any other island, Country, Territory, or place whatever, in like Manner utterly abolished, prohibited, and declared to be unlawful; and if any of His majesties Subjects, or any Person or persons resident within this *United Kingdom*, or any of the Islands, Colonies, Dominions, or Territories thereto belonging, or in His Majesties Occupation or Possession, shall, from and after the Day aforesaid, by him or themselves, or by his or their Factors or Agents or otherwise howsoever , deal or trade in, purchase, sell, barter, or transfer, or contract or agree for the dealing or trading in, purchasing, selling, bartering, or transferring of any Slave or Slaves, or any Person or persons intended to be sold, transferred, used, or dealt with as a Slave or Slaves contrary to the Prohibitions of this Act, he or they so offending shall forfeit and pay for every such Offence the Sum of One hundred Pounds of lawful Money of *Great Britain* for each and every Slave so purchased, sold, bartered, or transferred,

or contracted or agreed for as aforesaid, the One
Moiety thereof to the Use of His Majesty, His Heirs
and Successors, and the other Moiety to the Use of
any Person who shall inform, sue, and prosecute
for the same.

2.   And be it further enacted, that from and after the
said First Day of May One Thousand Eight
Hundred and Seven, it shall be unlawful for any of
His Majesty's Subjects, or any Person or persons
resident within this United Kingdom, or any of the
Islands, Colonies, Dominions, or Territories thereto
belonging, or in His Majesty's Possession or
Occupation, to fit out, man, or navigate, or to
procure to be fitted out, manned, or navigated, or
to be concerned in the fitting out manning, or
navigating, or in the procuring to be fitted out,
manned, or navigated, any Ship or Vessel for the
Purpose of assisting in, or being, employed in the
carrying on of the African Slave Trade, or in any
other the Dealing, Trading, or Concerns hereby
prohibited and declared to be unlawful, and every
Ship or Vessel which shall, from and after the Day
aforesaid, be fitted out, manned, navigated, used,
or employed by any such Subject or Subjects, person
or Persons, or on his or their Account, or by his or
their Assistance or procurement for any of the
Purposes aforesaid, and by this Act prohibited,
together with all her Boats, Guns, Tackle, Apparel,
and Furniture, shall become forfeited, and may and
shall be seized and prosecuted as herein-after is
mentioned and provided.

3.   And be it further enacted, That from and after the
said First Day of May, One thousand eight hundred
and seven, it shall be unlawful for any of His
Majesty's Subjects, or any Person or persons,
resident in this United Kingdom, or in any of the
Colonies, Territories, or Dominions thereunto

belonging or in His Majesty's Possession, or
Occupation, to carry away or remove, or knowingly
and willfully to procure, aid, or assist in the carrying
away or removing, as Slaves, or for the purpose of
being sold, transferred, used, or dealt with as Slaves,
any of the Subjects or Inhabitants of *Africa*, or any
Island, Country, Territory, or place in the *West Indies*,
or any part of *America* whatsoever, not being in the
Dominion, Possession, or Occupation of his
Majesty, either immediately or by Trans-shipment
at Sea or otherwise, directly or indirectly from Africa
or from any such island, Country, Territory, or place
as aforesaid, to any other island, Country, Territory,
or place whatever, and that it shall also be unlawful
for any of His Majesty's Subjects, or any Person or
Person's resident in this United Kingdom, or in any
of the Colonies, Territories, or Dominions thereunto
belonging, or in His Majesty's Possession or
Occupation, knowingly and willfully to receive,
detain, or confine on board, or to be aiding,
assisting, or concerned in the receiving, detaining,
or confining on board of any Ship or Vessel
whatever, any such Subject or Inhabitants aforesaid,
for the Purpose of his or her being so carried away
or removed as aforesaid, or of his or her being sold,
transferred used, or dealt with as a Slave, in any
Place or Country whatever; and if any Subject or
Inhabitant, Subjects or Inhabitants of *Africa*, or of
any Island, Country, Territory, or Place in the *West
Indies* or *America*, not being in the Dominion,
Possession, or Occupation of His Majesty, shall from
and after the Day aforesaid, be so unlawfully carried
away or removed, detained, confined, trans-shipped,
or received on board of any Ship or Vessel belonging
in the Whole or in Part to, or employed by any
Subject of His Majesty, or Person residing in His
Majesty's Dominions or Colonies, or any Territory

belonging to or in the Occupation of His Majesty, for any of the unlawful Purposes aforesaid, contrary to the Force and Effect, true Intent and Meaning of the Prohibitions in this Act contained, every such ship or Vessel in which any such person or Persons shall be so unlawfully carried away or removed, detained, confined, trans-shipped, or received on board for any of the said unlawful Purposes, together with all her Boats, Guns, tackle, Apparel, and Furniture, shall be forfeited, and all Property or pretended Property in any Slaves or Natives of Africa so unlawfully carried away or removed, detained, confined, trans-shipped or received on board, shall also be forfeited, and the same respectively shall and may be seized and prosecuted as herein-after is mentioned and provided; and every Subject of His Majesty, or Person resident within this United Kingdom, or any of the Islands, Colonies, Dominions, or Territories thereto belonging, or in His Majesty's Possession or Occupation who shall, as Owner, part Owner, Freighter or Shipper, Factor or Agent, Captain, Mate, Supercargo, or Surgeon, so unlawfully carry away, or assisting, detain, confine, trans-ship, or receive on board, or be aiding or assisting in the carrying away, removing, detaining, confining, trans-shipping, or receiving on board for any of the unlawful Purposes aforesaid, any such Subject or Inhabitant of Africa, or of any Island, Country, Territory, or Place, not being in the Dominion, Possession, or Occupation of His Majesty, shall forfeit and pay for each and every Slave or person so unlawful carried away, removed, detained, confined, trans-shipped, or received on board, the Sum of one hundred Pounds of lawful Money of *Great Britain*, One Moiety thereof to the Use of His Majesty, and the other Moiety to the Use of any

Person who shall inform, sue, and prosecute for the same.

4. And be it further enacted, That if any Subject or inhabitant, Subjects or Inhabitants of Africa, or of any Island, Country, Territory, or Place, not being in the Dominion, possession, or Occupation of his Majesty, who shall, at any Time from and after the Day aforesaid, have been unlawfully carried away or removed from Africa, or from any island, Country, Territory, or place, in the *West Indies* or *America*, not being in the Dominion, Possession, or Occupation of His Majesty, contrary to any of the Prohibitions or Provisions in this Act contained, shall be imported or brought into any island, Colony, Plantation, or territory, in the Dominion, possession, or Occupation of his Majesty, and there sold or disposed of as a Slave or Slaves, or placed, detained, or kept in a State of Slavery, such Subject or Inhabitant, Subjects or Inhabitants, so unlawfully carried away, or removed and imported, shall and may be seized and prosecuted, as forfeited to His Majesty, by such Person or persons, in such Courts, and in such Manner and Form, as any Goods or merchandize unlawfully imported into the same Island, Colony, Plantation, or Territory, may now be seized and prosecuted therein, by virtue of any Act or Acts of parliament now in force for regulating the Navigation and Trade of his Majesty's Colonies and Plantations, and shall and may, after his or their Condemnation, be disposed of in Manner hereinafter mentioned and provided.

5. And be it further enacted, That from and after the said First Day of May One Thousand eight hundred and seven, all Insurances whatsoever to be effected upon or in respect to any of the trading, dealing, carrying, removing, trans-shipping, or other Transactions by this Act prohibited, shall be also

prohibited and declared to be unlawful; and if any of His Majesty's Subjects, or any Person or Persons resident within this United Kingdom, or within any of the Islands, Colonies, Dominions, or Territories thereunto belonging, or in His Majesty's Possession or Occupation, shall knowingly and willfully subscribe, effect, or make, or cause or procure to be subscribed, effected, or made, any such unlawful Insurances or Insurance, he or they shall forfeit and pay for every such Offence the Sum of One hundred Pounds for every such Insurance, and also Treble the Amount paid or agreed to be paid as the Premium of any such Insurance, the One Moiety thereof to the Use of His Majesty, His Heirs and Successors, and the other Moiety to the Use of any Person who shall inform, sue, and prosecute for the same.

6. Provided always, That nothing herein contained shall extend, or be deemed or construed to extend, to prohibit or render unlawful the dealing or trading in the Purchase, Sale, barter, or Transfer, or the carrying away or removing for the Purpose of being sold, transferred, used, or dealt with as Slaves, or the detaining or confining for the Purpose of being so carried away or removed, of any Slaves which shall be exported, carried, or removed from Africa, in any Ship or Vessel which, on or before the said First Day of May One thousand eight hundred and seven, shall have been lawfully cleared out from Great Britain according to the Law now in force for regulating the carrying of Slaves from Africa, or to prohibit or render unlawful the manning or navigating any such Ship or Vessel, or to make void any Insurance thereon, so as the Slaves to be carried therein shall be finally landed in the West Indies on or before the First Day of March One thousand eight hundred and eight, unless prevented by

Capture, the Loss of the Vessel, by the Appearance of an Enemy upon the Coast, or other unavoidable Necessity, the Proof whereof shall lie upon the Coast, or other unavoidable Necessity, the proof whereof shall lie upon the Party charged; any Thing hereinbefore contained to the contrary notwithstanding.

7. And whereas it may happen, That during the present or future Wars, Ships or Vessels may be seized or detained as Prize, on board whereof Slaves or natives of *Africa*, carried and detained as Slaves, being the Property of His Majesty's Enemies, or otherwise liable to Condemnation as Prize of War, may be taken or found, and it is necessary to direct in what manner such Slaves or natives of *Africa* shall be hereafter treated and disposed of: And whereas it is also necessary to direct and provide for the Treatment and Disposal of any Slaves or natives of *Africa* carried, removed, treated or dealt with as Slaves, who shall be unlawfully carried away or removed contrary to the Prohibitions aforesaid, or any of them, and shall be afterwards found on board any Ship or Vessel liable to Seizure under this Act, or any other Act of parliament made for restraining or prohibiting the *African* Slave Trade, or shall be elsewhere lawfully seized as forfeited under this or any other such Act of Parliament as aforesaid; and it is expedient to encourage the Captors, Seizors, and Prosecutors thereof; be it therefore further enacted. That all Slaves and all Natives of *Africa*, treated, dealt with, carried, kept, or detained as Slaves which shall at any Time from and after the said First Day of May next be seized or taken as Prize of War, or liable to Forfeiture, under this or any other Act of Parliament made for restraining or prohibiting the *African* Slave Trade, shall and may, for the Purposes only of Seizure, Prosecution, and Condemnation as Prize or as Forfeitures, be

considered, treated, taken, and adjudged as Slaves and property in the same manner as Negro Slaves have been heretofore considered, treated, taken, and adjudged, when seized as Prize of War, or as forfeited for any Offence against the Laws of Trade and Navigation respectively, but the same shall be condemned as Prize of War, or as forfeited to the sole Use of His Majesty, His Heirs and Successors, for the Purpose only of divesting and bearing all other Property, Right, Title, or Interest whatever, which before existed, or might afterwards be set up or claimed in or to such Slaves or natives of *Africa* to seized, prosecuted, and condemned; and the fame nevertheless shall in no case be liable to be sold, disposed of, treated or dealt with as Slaves, by or on the Part of His Majesty, His Heirs or Successors, or by or on the Part of any Person or persons claiming or to claim from, by, or under His Majesty, His Heirs and Successors, or under or by force of any such Sentence or Condemnation: Provided always, that it shall be lawful for His Majesty, His Heirs and Successors, and such Officers, Civil or Military, as shall, by any General or Special Order of the King in Council, be from Time to Time appointed and empowered to receive, protect, and provide for such Natives of Africa as shall be so condemned, either to enter and enlist the same, or any of them, into His Majesty's Land or Sea Service, as Soldiers, Seamen, or Marines, or to bind the same, or any of them, whether of full Age or not, as Apprentices, for any Term not exceeding Fourteen Years, to such Person or Persons, in such Place or Places, and upon such Terms and Conditions, and subject to such Regulations, as to His Majesty shall seem meet, and shall by any General of Special Order of His Majesty in Council be in that Behalf directed and appointed; and any Indenture of Apprenticeship duly made and executed, by any Person or person to be for the Purpose appointed by any such Order in Council, for any Term not exceeding Fourteen Years, shall be of the same Force and Effect as if the party thereby bound as an Apprentice had himself or herself, when of full Age upon good Consideration, duly executed the same; and every such Native of *Africa* who shall be so enlisted or entered as aforesaid into any of His Majesty's Land or Sea Forces as a Soldier, Seaman, or Marine, shall be considered, treated, and dealt with in all respects as if he had voluntarily so enlisted or entered himself.

8.   Provided also, and be it further enacted, That where any Slaves or Natives of *Africa*, taken as Prize or War by any of His Majesty's Ships of War, or privateers duly commissioned, shall be finally condemned as such to His Majesty's Use as aforesaid, there shall be paid to the Captors thereof by the Treasurer of His Majesty's Navy, in like Manner as the Bounty called Head Money is now paid by virtue of an Act of Parliament, made in the Forty-fifth Year of His Majesty's Reign, intituled, An Act for the Encouragement of Seamen, and for the better and more effectually manning His Majesty's Navy during the present War, such Bounty as His Majesty, His Heirs and Successors, shall have directed by any Order in Council, so as the same shall not exceed the Sum of Forty Pounds lawful Money of *Great Britain* for every Man, or Thirty Pounds of like Money for every Woman, or Ten Pounds of like Money for every Child or Person not above Fourteen Years old, that shall be so taken and condemned, and shall be delivered over in good Health to the proper Officer or Officers, Civil or Military, so appointed as aforesaid to receive, protect, and provide for the same; which Bounties

shall be divided amongst the Officers, Seamen, Marines, and Soldiers on Board His Majesty's Ships of War, or hired armed Ships, in Manner, Form, and proportion, as by His Majesty's Proclamation for granting the Distribution of Prizes already issued, or to be issued for the Purpose is or shall be directed and appointed, and amongst the Owners, Officers, and Seamen of any private Ship or Vessel of War, in such Manner and Proportion as, by an Agreement in Writing that they shall have entered into for that Purpose, shall be directed.

9. Provided always, and be it further enacted, That in order to entitle the Captors to receive the said Bounty Money, the Numbers of men, Women, and Children, so taken, condemned, and delivered over, shall be proved to the Commissioners of His Majesty's Navy, by producing, instead of the Oaths and Certificates prescribed by the said Act as to Head Money, a Copy, duly certified, of the Sentence or Decree of Condemnation, whereby the Numbers of men, Women, and Children, so taken and condemned, shall appear to have been distinctly proved; and also, by producing a Certificate under the Hand of the said Officer or Officers, Military or Civil, so appointed as aforesaid, and to whom the same shall have been delivered, acknowledging that he or they hath or have received the same, to be disposed of according to His Majesty's Instructions and regulations as aforesaid.

10. Provided also, and be it further inacted, That in any Cases in which Doubts shall arise whether the party or parties claiming such Bounty Money is or are entitled thereto, the same shall be summarily determined by the Judge of the High Court of Admiralty, or by the Judge of any Court of Admiralty in which the prize shall have been adjudged, subject nevertheless to an Appeal to the

lord Commissioners of Appeals in Prize Causes.

11. Provided also, and be it further enacted, That on the Condemnation to the Use of his Majesty, His heirs and Successors, in Manner aforesaid, of any Slaves or Natives of *Africa,* seized and prosecuted as forfeited for any Offence against this Act, or any other Act of Parliament made for the restraining or prohibiting the African Slave Trade (except in the Case of Seizures made at Sea by the Commanders or Officers of His Majesty's Ships or Vessels or War) there shall be paid to and to the Use of the Person who shall have sued, informed, and prosecuted the same to Condemnation, the Sums of Thirteen Pounds lawful Money aforesaid for every Man, of Ten Pounds like Money for every Woman, and of Three Pounds like Money for every Child or person under the Age of Fourteen Years, that shall be so condemned and delivered over in good Health to the said Civil or military Officer so to be appointed to receive, protect, and provide for the same, and also the like Sums to and to Use of the Governor or Commander in Chief of any Colony or plantation wherein such Seizure shall have been made; but in Cases of any such Seizures made at Sea by the Commanders or Officers of His Majesty's Ships or Vessels of War, for Forfeiture under this Act, or any other Act of Parliament made for the restraining or prohibiting the *African* Slave Trade, there shall be paid to the Commander of Officer who shall so seize, inform, and prosecute for every man so condemned and delivered over, the Sum of Twenty Pounds like Money, for every Woman the Sum of Fifteen Pounds like Money, and for every Child or person under the Age of Fourteen Years the Sum of Five Pounds like Money, subject nevertheless to such Distribution of the said Bounties or rewards for the said Seizures made at Sea as His Majesty,

His Heirs and Successors, shall think fit to order and direct by any other Order of Council made for that Purpose; for all which Payments so to be made as Bounties or rewards upon Seizures and Prosecutions for Offences against this Act, or any other Act of Parliament made for restraining the African Slave Trade, the officer or Officers, Civil or Military, so to be appointed as aforesaid to receive, protect, and provide for such Slaves or Natives of Africa so to be condemned and delivered over, shall, after the Condemnation and Receipt thereof as aforesaid, grant Certificates in favour of the Governor and Party seizing, informing, and prosecuting as aforesaid respectively, or the latter alone (as the Case may be) addressed to the Lords Commissioners of his Majesty's Treasury; who, upon the Production to them of any such Certificate, and of an authentic Copy, duly certified, of the Sentence of Condemnation of the said Slaves or *Africans* to His Majesty's Use as aforesaid, and also of a Receipt under the Hand of such Officer or Officers so appointed as aforesaid, specifying that such Slaves or *Africans* have by him or them been received in good Health as aforesaid, shall direct Payment to be made from and out of the Consolidated Fund of *Great Britain* of the Amount of the Monies specified in such Certificate, to the lawful Holders of the fame, or the Persons entitled to the Benefit thereof respectively.

12. And be it further enacted, That if any Person shall willfully and fraudulently forge or counterfeit any such Certificate, Copy of Sentence of Condemnation, or Receipt as aforesaid, or any Part thereof, or shall knowingly and willfully utter or publish the same, knowing it to be forged or counterfeited, with Intent to defraud His Majesty, His Heirs and Successors, or any other Person or

Persons whatever, the Party so offending shall, on Conviction, suffer Death as in Cases of Felony, without Benefit of Clergy.

13. And be it further enacted, That the several Pecuniary Penalties or Forfeitures imposed and inflicted by this Act, shall and may be sued for, prosecuted, and recovered in any Court of Record in *Great Britain,* or in any Court of Record or Vice Admiralty in any Part of His Majesty's Dominions wherein the Offence was committed, or where the Offender may be found after the Commission of such Offence; and that in all Cases of Seizure of any Ships, Vessels, Slaves or pretended Slaves, Goods or Effects, for any Forfeiture under this Act, the same shall and may respectively be sued for; prosecuted and recovered in any Court of Record in *Great Britain* or in any Court of Record or Vice Admiralty in any Part of His Majesty's Dominions in or nearest to which such Seizures may be made, or to which such Ships or Vessels, Slaves or pretended Slaves, Goods or Effects (if seized at Sea or without the Limits of any *British* Jurisdiction) may most conveniently be carried for Trial, and all the said Penalties and Forfeitures, whether pecuniary or specific (unless where it is expressly otherwise provided for by this Act) shall go and belong to such Person and Persons in such Shares and Proportions, and shall and may be sued for and prosecuted, tried, recovered, distributed, and applied in such and the like Manner and by the same Ways and Means, and subject to the same Rules and Directions, as any Penalties or Forfeitures incurred in *Great Britain,* and in the *British* Colonies or Plantations in *America* respectively, by force of any Act of Parliament relating to the Trade and Revenues of the said *British* Colonies or Plantations in *America,* now go and belong to, and

may now be sued for, prosecuted, tried, recovered, distributed and applied respectively in *Great Britain* or in the said Colonies or Plantations respectively, under and by virtue of a certain Act of Parliament made in the Fourth Year of His present Majesty, entitled:

An Act for granting certain Duties in the British *Colonies and Plantations in* America, *for continuing amending, and making perpetual an Act passed in the Sixth Year of the Reign of His late Majesty King* George *the second, entitled:*

"An Act for the better securing and encouraging the 'Trade of His Majesty's Sugar Colonies in America; *for applying the Produce of such Duties to arise by virtue of the said Act towards defraying the Expences of defending, protecting, and securing the said Colonies and Plantations;" for explaining an Act made in the Twenty-fifth Year of the Reign of King Charles the Second, entitled:*

"An Act for the Encouragement of the Greenland *and* Eastland *Trades, and for the better securing the Plantation trade, and for altering and disallowing several Drawbacks on Exports from the Kingdom, and more effectively presenting the clandestine Conveyance of Goods to and from the said Colonies and plantations, and improving and securing the Trade between the same and Great Britain."*

14. And be it further enacted, That all Ships and Vessels, Slaves or Natives of *Africa,* carried, conveyed, or dealt with as Slaves, and all other Goods and Effects that shall or may become forfeited for any Offence committed against this Act, shall and may be seized by any Officer of His Majesty's Customs or Excise, or by the Commanders or Officers of any of His Majesty's Ships or Vessels of War, who, in making and prosecuting any such Seizures, shall have the Benefit of all the Provisions made by the said Act of the Fourth Year of His present Majesty, or any other Act of Parliament

made for the Protection of Officers seizing and prosecuting for any Offence against the said Act, or any other Act of Parliament relating to the Trade and Revenues of the *British* Colonies or Plantations in *America*.

15. And be it further enacted, That all Offences committed against this Act may be inquired of, tried, determined, and dealt with as Misdemeanors, as if the Same had been respectively committed within the Body of the County of *Middlesex*.

16. Provided also, and be it further enacted, That it shall and may be lawful for his Majesty in Council, from Time to Time to make such Orders and Regulations for the future Disposal and Support of such Negroes as shall have been bound Apprentices under this Act, after the term of their Apprenticeship shall have expired, as to His Majesty shall seem meet, and as may prevent such Negroes from becoming at any Time chargeable upon the Island in which they shall have been so bound Apprentices as aforesaid.

17. Provided always, and be it further enacted, That none of the Provisions of any Act as to enlisting for any limited Period of Service, or as to any Rules or Regulations for the granting any Pensions or Allowances to any Soldiers discharged after certain Periods of Service, shall extend, or be deemed or construed in any Manner to extend, to any Negroes so enlisted and serving in any of His Majesty's Forces.

18. And be it further enacted, That if any Action or Suit shall be commenced either in *Great Britain* or elsewhere, against any Person or Persons for any Thing done in pursuance of this Act, the Defendant or Defendants in such Action or Suit may plead the General Issue, and give this Act and the Special Matter in Evidence at any Trial to be had thereupon,

and that the same was done in pursuance and by the Authority of this Act; and if it shall appear so to have been done, the Jury shall find for the Defendant or Defendants; and if the Plaintiff shall be nonsuited or discontinue his Action after the Defendant or Defendants shall have appeared, or if Judgement shall be given upon any Verdict or Demurrer against the Plaintiff, the Defendant or Defendants shall recover Treble Costs and have the like Remedy for the same, as Defendants have in other Cases by Law.

Bibliography

An Act for the Abolition of the Slave Trade. London: George Eyre & Andrew Strahan, Printers to the King's Most Excellent Majesty, 1807.

Anstey, Roger. *The Atlantic Slave Trade and British Abolition*. Atlantic Highlands: NJ Humanities Press, 1975.

Augier, Roy, S.C. Gordon, D.G. Hall and M. Reckford. *The Making of the West Indies* Trinidad and Jamaica: Longmans, 1982.

Beckles, Hilary, and Verene Shepherd. *Liberties Lost: Caribbean Indigenous Societies and Slave Systems*. Cambridge: Cambridge University Press, 2004.

Beckles, Hilary. 'Emancipation by Law or War? Wilberforce and the 1816 Barbados Slave Rebellion'. In *Abolition and Its Aftermath*, ed. D. Richardson. London: Frank Cass, 1985. 80-110.

Blackburn, Robin. *The Making of New World Slavery: From the Baroque to the Modern, 1492–1800*. London and New York: Verso, 1997.

— — —. *The Overthrow of Colonial slavery, 1776–1848*. New York: Verso, 1988.

Bush, Barbara. *Slave Women in Caribbean Society, 1650–1838*. Kingston and London: Heinemann Publishers (Caribbean) and James Currey, 1990.

Cohen, William. *The French Encounter with Africans: White Responses to Blacks, 1530–1880*. Bloomington: Indiana University Press, 1980.

Conrad, Peter. *The Destruction of Brazilian Slavery*. Berkeley: University of California Press, 1972.

Craton, Michael. *Testing the Chains: Resistance to Slavery in the British West Indies*. Ithaca [N.Y.]: Cornell University Press, 1982.

Curtin, Philip. *The Atlantic Slave Trade: A Census*. Madison: University of Wisconsin Press, 1969.

— — —. *Economic Change in Pre-Colonial Africa: Senegambia in the Era of the Slave Trade*. Madison: University of Wisconsin, 1975. Reprint. Ithaca, NY: Cornell University Press, 1982.

Davis, David Brion. *Slavery and Human Progress*. New York: Oxford University Press, 1984.

— — —. *Slavery and Western Culture*. Ithaca, NY: Cornell University Press, 1966.

Drescher, Seymour. *Capitalism and Anti-Slavery*. New York: Oxford University Press, 1984.

— — —. *Econocide: British Slavery in the Era of Abolition*. Pittsburgh: University of Pittsburgh Press, 1977.

Eltis, David. *The Rise of African Slavery in the Americas*. Cambridge: Cambridge University Press, 2000.

Eltis, David, Stephen Behrendt, Herbert Klein and David Richardson. *The Trans-Atlantic Slave Trade: A Database on CD-ROM*. Cambridge: Cambridge University Press, 1999.

Eltis, David. 'Traffic in slaves Between British West Indian Colonies, 1807–1833'. *Economic History Review* 25 (1972): 55–64

Engerman, Stanley, and Joseph Inikori, eds. *The Atlantic Slave Trade: Effects on Economies, Societies, and Peoples in Africa, the Americas and Europe*. Chapel Hill, 1991.

Finley, Moses. *Ancient Slavery and Modern Ideology*. New York: Viking Press, 1981.

Geggus, David. 'Slavery, War, and Revolution in the Greater Caribbean, 1789–1815'. In *A Turbulent Time: The French Revolution and the Greater Caribbean*, eds. David Gaspar and David Geggus. Gainesville: University of Florida Press, 1997. 1-50.

Gomez, Michael. 'A Quality of Anguish: The Igbo Response to Enslavement in the Americas'. In *Trans-Atlantic Dimensions of Ethnicity in the African Diaspora*, eds. Paul E. Lovejoy and David V. Trotman. London: Continuum, 2003. 82-95

Goveia, Elsa. 'Amelioration and Emancipation in the British Caribbean'. Mona, Kingston: Department of History, University of the West Indies, 1977.

— — —. *Slave Society in the British Leeward Islands at the end of the Eighteenth Century*. New Haven: Yale University Press, 1965.

Higman, Barry W. *Slave Populations of the British Caribbean, 1807–1834*. Baltimore: The Johns Hopkins University Press, 1984.

House of Lords, London. *Act for the Abolition of the Slave Trade. 1807.*

House of Lords, London. *Order-in-Council, 1806.*

Inikori, Joseph. *Africans and the Industrial Revolution in England: A Study in International and Economic Development*. Cambridge: Cambridge University Press, 2002.

— — —, ed. *Forced Migration: The Impact of the Export Slave Trade on African Societies*. New York: Africana Publishing Co. 1982.

Jakobsson, Stiv. *Am I not a Man and a Brother? British Missionaries and the Abolition of the Slave Trade and Slavery in West Africa and the West Indies 1786-1838*. Lund: Gleerup, 1972.

Jamaica National Heritage Trust. *Tacky Freedom Fighter & Leader of the 1760 Enslaved Revolt*. Kingston: Jamaica National Heritage

Trust, 2006.

James, C.L.R. *The Black Jacobins*. London: Secker and Warburg, 1938.

Jennings, Judith. *The Business of Abolishing the British Slave Trade, 1783–1807*. London: Portland, 1997.

Jennings, Lawrence. *French Anti-Slavery*. Cambridge: Cambridge University Press, 2000.

John, A. Meredith. *The Plantation Slaves of Trinidad, 1783–1816*. Cambridge: Cambridge University Press, 1988.

Law, Robin. *The Oyo Empire*. Oxford: Oxford University Press, 1977.

— — —. *The Slave Coast of West Africa, 1550–1750: The Impact of the Atlantic Slave Trade on an African Society*. Oxford: Oxford University Press, 1991.

Locke, Mary. *Anti-Slavery in America*. Boston: Ginn, 1901, 1968. Reprint.

Lovejoy, Paul E. *Transformations in Slavery: A History of Slavery in Africa*. Cambridge: Cambridge University Press, 2000.

McGowan, Winston. 'African Resistance to the Atlantic Slave Trades in Africa'. In *Slavery and Abolition* 11 (1990): 5–29

Martin, S.I. *Britain's Slave Trade*. London: Channel 4 Books, 1999.

Midgley, Clare. *Women against Slavery: The British Campaigns, 1780–1870*. London and New York: Routledge, 1992.

Miers, Suzanne. *Britain and the Ending of the Slave Trade*. London: Longman Publishers, 1975.

Morgan, Edmund. *American Slavery: American Freedom: the ordeal of colonial Virginia*. New York: Norton Publishers, 1975.

— — —. 'Slavery and Freedom: The American Paradox'. *Journal of American History* 59 (1972):5-29

Mullin, Michael. *Africa in America: Slave Acculuration and Resistance in the American South and the British Caribbean 1736-1831*. Urbana: University of Illinois Press, 1992.

Murray, David. *Odious Commerce: Britain, Spain, and the Abolition of the Cuban Slave Trade*. Cambridge: Cambridge University Press, 1980.

Patterson Orlando. *Slavery and Social Death: A Comparative Study*. Cambridge: Cambridge University Press, 1982.

Pope-Hennessey, James. *Sins of our Fathers: A Study of the Atlantic Slave Traders, 1441–1807*. London: Weidenfeld and Nicholson, 1967.

Ragatz, Lowell, *The Fall of the Planter class in The British Caribbean, 1763–1833*. New York: Octagon Books, 1977.

Rathbone, Richard. 'Some Thoughts on Resistance to Enslavement in West Africa'. *Slavery and Abolition* 6 (1985):11–22.

Rodney, Walter. *How Europe Underdeveloped Africa*. London: Bogle L'ouverture, 1988.

Roberts, George. 'Movement in Slave Populations of the Caribbean during the Period of Slave Registration'. In *Comparative Perspectives on Slavery in the New World Plantation Societies*, eds. V. Rubin and A. Tuden. New York: Annals of the New York Academy of Sciences, 1977: 145-186.

Shepherd, Verene, and Hilary Beckles, eds. *Caribbean Slavery in the Atlantic World*. Kingston: Ian Randle Publishers, 2000.

Thomas, Hugh. *The Slave Trade: A History of the Atlantic Slave Trade, 1440 1870*. London: Simon & Schuster, 1997.

Thompson, Alvin. *Flight to Freedom: African Runaways and Maroons in the Americas*. Mona, Kingston: University of the West Indies Press, 2006.

Ward, J.R. *British West Indian Slavery, 1750–1834*. Oxford, England: Oxford University Press, 1988.

Williams, Eric. *Capitalism and Slavery*. London: André Deutsch Ltd., 1964. Reprint. Kingston: Ian Randle Publishers, 2004.

— — —. 'The British West Indian Slave Trade after its Abolition in 1807'. *Journal of Negro History* 27 (1942): 175-191.

Websites for Illustrative Material

http://www.pbs.org/wgbh/aia/part2/2h67.html
'Am I Not a Man and a Brother?' Image Credit: Reproduced with the kind permission of the Trustees of The Wedgwood Museum, Barlaston, Staffordshire, England.

http://www.nationalarchives.gov.uk/pathways/blackhistory/rights/abolition.htm
'Am I Not a Woman and a Sister?'

http://www.brycchancarey.com/equiano/
Portrait of Equiano.

http://www.brycchancarey.com/sancho/
Thomas Gainsborough's portrait of Sancho, painted in Bath in
   1768.
http://website.lineone.net/~stkittsnevis/act_of_1807.htm

Abolition Act, 1807.
http://www.spartacus.schoolnet.co.uk

Images of William Wilberforce, Thomas Clarkson,
and Granville Sharp)
http://www.anointedlinks.com/amazing_grace.html

Image of John Newton
http://www.wwnorton.com/college/history/ralph/resource/
   22slaves.htm

Image of Brooks Slave Ship: Photo Credit: The
Warder Collection, NY.

http://www.cyberhymnal.org/htm/a/m/amazgrac.htm